Building Trust in Diverse Teams

The Toolkit for Emergency Response

Acknowledgements

The Emergency Capacity Building Project

Building Trust in Diverse Teams: the Toolkit for Emergency Response was produced as part of the Emergency Capacity Building (ECB) Project. The ECB Project is a collaborative effort of the seven agencies of the Inter-agency Working Group on Emergency Capacity: CARE International, Catholic Relief Services, the International Rescue Committee, Mercy Corps, Oxfam GB, Save the Children, and World Vision International. These agencies and their partners are jointly addressing issues of staff capacity, accountability and impact measurement, risk reduction, and the use of information and communication technologies (ICTs) in emergencies, with the goal of improving the speed, quality, and effectiveness of the humanitarian community in saving the lives, safeguarding the livelihoods, and protecting the rights of people affected by emergencies. For further information, please visit www.ecbproject.org or email info@ecbproject.org.

Funding for the Emergency Capacity Building Project was provided by the Bill & Melinda Gates Foundation and the Microsoft Corporation. Without their commitment to improve the capacity of the humanitarian sector, this book would not have been possible. We thank them for their generous support.

Key contributors

The production of this book is the culmination of a tremendous global collaborative effort that would not have been possible without the time and commitment of the individuals listed below.

Building Trust in Diverse Teams Working Group

A very special thanks to the Building Trust in Diverse Teams Working Group for providing overall strategic leadership from the point of conceptualisation of the project to hands-on testing of tools and completion of the toolkit, on top of already demanding roles within their respective agencies.

Lisa Smith, Toolkit Manager, CARE International

Stephen Claborne, Mercy Corps

Amy Bess, Building Trust in Diverse Teams Project Manager, Oxfam GB

Bimla Ojelay-Surtees, Project Leader, Oxfam GB

Jo-Ann Simmons, Save the Children

Gisla Dewey, World Vision International

Country offices

We want to thank the Country Directors for providing in-country support to the consultants and Working Group to test and refine the assessment and trust-building tools.

Cecily Bryant, CARE Malawi Country Director

Nick Osborne, CARE Sri Lanka Country Director

Josh deWald, Mercy Corps Sri Lanka Country Director

Sanjay Awasthi, Oxfam Malawi Country Programme Manager

Joan Summers, Oxfam Sri Lanka Country Programme Manager

Paul Mecartney, Save the Children Malawi Country Director

Mulugeta Abebe, World Vision Malawi Director

Marion Chindongo, World Vision Malawi Associate Director

Perry Mansfield, World Vision Sri Lanka

Consultants

We want to thank the three consultants for sharing their expertise in trust and assisting with shaping the research into practical tools for emergency-response teams. We also thank them for going beyond their remit by providing additional support to ensure that the tools were of the highest calibre.

Nigel Ewington, TCO International Diversity Management

Dennis Hamilton, Training Associates Pacific

Richard Lowe, Castleton Partners

Building Trust in Diverse Teams Project Champions

We want to thank the senior managers across the five ECB organisations who served as 'champions' of this Project. Without their commitment and recognition that trust matters, we would not have been able to embark upon this work.

Heather Brooks, CARE International

Collins Dobbs, Consultant (former CARE International)

Patrick Solomon, CARE International

Mignon Mazique, Mercy Corps

Susan Romanski, Mercy Corps

Christine Newton, Oxfam GB

Ivan Scott, Oxfam GB

Cynthia Carr, Save the Children

Meredith Richardson, former Save the Children

Susan Barber, World Vision International

ECB Project staff

We thank the ECB Project staff for their role in providing overall project support, from acting as mentors to practical help with logistics.

Aziza Abdurazakova, Project Officer

Matt Bannermann, Project Director and Communications Manager

Greg Brady, Project Director

Mark Hammersley, Staff Capacity Initiative Manager

Anna Hiltunen, Project Assistant

Bruce Russell, Project Assistant

We would also like to thank the 44 staff in Sri Lanka and 55 staff in Malawi who took part in providing critical and substantive feedback on the Trust Index and the trust-building tools.

Building Trust in Diverse Teams

The Toolkit for Emergency Response

Cover image: © iStockPhoto/Gary Woodard

First published by Oxfam GB for the Emergency Capacity Building Project in 2007

© Oxfam GB for the Emergency Capacity Building Project 2007

ISBN 978-0-85598-615-5

A catalogue record for this publication is available from the British Library.

Available from:

Bournemouth English Book Centre, PO Box 1496, Parkstone, Dorset, BH12 3YD, UK
tel: +44 (0)1202 712933; fax: +44 (0)1202 712930; email: oxfam@bebc.co.uk

USA: Stylus Publishing LLC, PO Box 605, Herndon, VA 20172-0605, USA
tel: +1 (0)703 661 1581; fax: +1 (0)703 661 1547; email: styluspub@aol.com

For details of local agents and representatives in other countries, consult our website:
www.oxfam.org.uk/publications
or contact Oxfam Publishing, Oxfam House, John Smith Drive, Cowley, Oxford, OX4 2JY, UK
tel +44 (0) 1865 472255; fax (0) 1865 472393; email: publish@oxfam.org.uk

Our website contains a fully searchable database of all our titles, and facilities for secure on-line ordering.

Published by Oxfam GB, Oxfam House, John Smith Drive, Cowley, Oxford, OX4 2JY, UK

Printed by Information Press, Eynsham

Inners printed on recycled paper made from 100% post-consumer waste.

Cover printed on FSC accredited 75% recycled paper.

Oxfam GB is a registered charity, no. 202 918, and is a member of Oxfam International.

Contents

Preface

What is trust? Why it is important in team performance? What increases or decreases the level of trust in a team? How can leaders build high levels of trust and effectively manage trust in a team?

A plethora of books and articles have been written to address these questions, but they are primarily for use in business settings. Traditionally, humanitarian organisations have integrated some of this thinking into their leadership trainings, diversity curriculum, and preparedness planning. However, until now, there has not been a concerted effort to create a body of knowledge about trust as it specifically applies to diverse teams in a humanitarian emergency setting.

The Emergency Capacity Building Project (ECB – see Acknowledgements) commissioned research by McKinsey & Company and found that staff in the field and at agency headquarters identified a culture of trust between national and international staff as one of the most important staffing factors in agencies' ability to launch timely and effective emergency responses. As a result, the seven large international development organisations which make up ECB have drawn on their collective expertise and have endeavored to address the questions in the first paragraph above, as they relate to the humanitarian context. Five of the seven ECB agencies formed a Building Trust in Diverse Teams Working Group to design and implement a project to address this key issue and identify practical approaches and tools to improve levels of trust in teams.

This toolkit is the culmination of several stages of work of the Building Trust Project. The first step was to establish how humanitarian aid workers defined trust. The Building Trust Working Group commissioned Castleton Partners and TCO International Diversity Management, a partnership of two UK-based consulting groups specialising in the topic of trust, to research the definition of trust by reviewing available literature and interviewing staff across the seven ECB agencies. The research resulted in a definition that outlined ten criteria for trust (described on pages 9–12). It then led to the development of a tool to measure trust, the Trust Index (pages 22–34), which maps out factors that influence levels of trust.

Next, action research carried out with staff from five of the ECB agencies in Sri Lanka and Malawi led to the refinement of the Trust Index and helped to define the types of tools that could help diverse teams build trust. After careful work on tool development by Castleton Partners and TCO International Diversity Management and the Working Group, the tools were then tried out and further refined with the teams in Sri Lanka and Malawi.

Through each step of the process, the Working Group has been dedicated to involving field staff in reviewing, revising, and validating each of the tools presented in this toolkit. Their participation and inclusion in the process has helped to ensure that the tools will be relevant and will improve emergency-response efforts. There are considerable differences between Malawi and Sri Lanka in terms of culture and the nature of the emergency setting, but in fact both the similarity and diversity of the staff responses from each country have served to strengthen the tools. The enthusiasm and valuable feedback from staff have not only validated the decision to focus on building trust in diverse teams, but have also offered real-time benefits to our staff who have already begun to weave some of the tools into their operating models and management practices. At field level in Sri Lanka and Malawi, for example, staff immediately realised that some of the tools were relevant and versatile enough to use beyond emergency response; they have included them in their development work both at team level and with communities and partners.

The trust work has also resonated at several of our head offices where human-resource personnel, diversity managers, and other key stakeholders have acknowledged that issues of trust need to be embedded in our organisational fabric before an emergency strikes. To this end, work has already started to integrate the trust tools into leadership-development programmes in some of the five ECB agencies involved in this project.

For us, the ECB agency members (Amy Bess [Project Manager], Stephen Claborne, Gisla Dewey, Jo-ann Simmons, Bimla Ojelay-Surtees, and Lisa Smith) that comprise the Building Trust in Diverse Teams Working Group, this collaborative experience has produced new working partnerships and reinforced the finding that investing in the issue of trust in a way that strengthens and builds effective teams is priceless, and massively increases the quality of work.

Our goal has been to create an accessible and versatile set of tools that will be used across the sector to improve team effectiveness during an emergency and to improve our ability to save lives – the primary driving force behind this work.

We hope that you will use these tools with this goal in mind.

Sincerely,

Bimla Ojelay-Surtees
Global Diversity Manager, Oxfam GB, and Project Leader, Building Trust Project

How to use this toolkit

This toolkit provides a framework and tools to support diverse teams to build a culture of trust throughout the cycle of an emergency response. The entire contents of the toolkit are also included on a CD in the back of the book.

The toolkit should be used by humanitarian practitioners, human-resource departments, country-office management teams, and head-office emergency professionals who seek comprehensive, accessible, and versatile tools for assessing, measuring, and building trust in teams.

The core components are located in Sections 2 (The Trust Index) and 4 (The trust-building tools), with informal activities in Section 5, and further resources and a glossary at the end.

The Trust Index should be used first, to assess the level of trust among team members and identify areas where levels of trust can be improved. The team should then create a trust-building plan, identifying appropriate measures to take, and tools to build trust in the team. The ten trust-building tools are grouped around components of the Trust Index and can be selected based on the identified trust needs as well as the stage of the emergency response. Each tool is divided into six sections: 1) Learning objective; 2) Overview; 3) Session plan; 4) How it works; 5) Facilitation tips; and 6) Links to the ten criteria for trust (NB Tools 7 and 8 do not include session plans, facilitation tips, or links to the ten criteria for trust as they are guidelines for managers rather than team-orientated tools).

The overall toolkit design employs user-friendly language and methodology that can be adapted to most local contexts. Given the time constraints involved at the onset of an emergency, these tools have been designed with 'breaks' so that if teams need to end an exercise due to work demands, they can stop and resume the tool later, safeguarding the purpose and integrity of the process. Teams can also extract relevant sections based on their needs and feel free to come back to other areas covered in this toolkit when necessary.

When teams have worked through the parts of the toolkit relevant for them, they should have a better understanding of how to identify behaviours that influence trust, and how to apply the necessary tools to build trust to improve team effectiveness.

1 • Defining trust

Why trust matters

The evidence

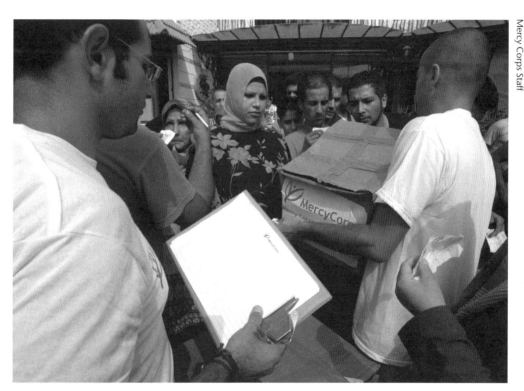

Southern Lebanon, June 2006 – distribution of basic supplies to families displaced by the cross-border fighting.

'Trust' is a vital ingredient for effective emergency-response teams. Research carried out by McKinsey and Company in 2006 on behalf of the Emergency Capacity Building Project (ECB) concluded that creating a 'culture of trust' amongst national and international staff was the *second most important factor* in creating effective emergency-response teams. They reached this conclusion after asking 102 managers from seven different agencies for their views on the most important staffing factors for emergency-response teams.

These initial findings were confirmed, extended, and elaborated in a second study carried out by Castleton Partners and TCO International Diversity Management during December 2006. They conducted in-depth interviews with 29 people from five different humanitarian agencies involved in the Building Trust Working Group – all well-experienced in emergency-response situations. The conclusion again was that trust between team members is essential if the team is to perform effectively in helping the beneficiaries and the local communities.

Much research on trust has also been carried out in other contexts including in the commercial sector. Although emergency-response teams face particular difficulties and pressures, many of the findings of this body of research in terms of why trust is important do also apply to emergency-response teams. There is now clear research evidence which shows strong links between the level of trust in a team or work group and:

- fuller and more effective co-operation and collaboration;
- higher levels of organisational commitment and morale;
- improved flexibility and lowering of co-ordination costs;
- quicker and better knowledge transfer between team members;
- increased productivity including in virtual teamwork;
- greater participation in decision-making processes and improved communication;
- higher levels of innovation and creativity in solving problems;
- easier support for change initiatives;
- enhanced leadership effectiveness;
- more effective working relationships.[1]

So what are the mechanisms by which high levels of trust produce these results? They are most easily identified in situations where mistrust prevails; low levels of trust affect productivity as people minimise their vulnerability by 'playing safe'. Ever more elaborate and costly checking systems are introduced, offers of advice are ignored, and valuable but sensitive information is withheld. Cultural differences in values, experience, and working practices become a source of stress, divisiveness, and mis-communication rather than an opportunity for valuing diversity and more creative decision-making. These circumstances, in turn, lead to communication breakdowns, defensiveness, poor team learning, and higher levels of anxiety and stress. Team energies are diverted away from the external needs of the beneficiaries.

Managing trust

In most teams, and most emergency-response teams, 'trust' is not often talked about explicitly. When it is, most people will agree that it is important but the conversation does not go much further. Contrast this with another vital resource in any team – finance. Modern management techniques have developed highly sophisticated ways of measuring and controlling the flows of money through organisations – including humanitarian agencies. Just as money facilitates the physical-task aspects of emergency-response team work, so, too, does trust facilitate the human relationships. However, no similar techniques exist for measuring trust. To manage and promote trust within an emergency-response team we need ways of measuring and enhancing it.

[1] See Emergency Capacity Building Project (2007) in Further resources

Measuring trust

As part of the ECB project, Castleton and TCO International Diversity Management identified ten 'criteria for trust'. These are the behaviours and approaches that can either build or destroy trust within an emergency-response team, and they provide the basis for measuring and managing trust within a team.

The ten criteria for trust are described in more detail on pages 9–12. They are:

1.	**Competence**	Trust based on a perception that team members are competent, and so will not let me down
2.	**Openness with information**	Trust based on the observation that other team members share information important to the team proactively and clearly
3.	**Integrity**	Trust based on the observation that other team members maintain promises, are team-orientated, and behave towards me in accordance with a moral code
4.	**Reciprocity**	Trust based on the observation that other team members are trusting and co-operative towards me
5.	**Compatibility**	Trust based on background, values, approaches, interests, and objectives held in common
6.	**Goodwill**	Trust based on the belief that other team members are concerned about my overall welfare
7.	**Predictability**	Trust based on the observation that the behaviour of team members is consistent over time and in different contexts
8.	**Well-being**	Trust arising from the feeling that I have nothing to fear from other members of the team
9.	**Inclusion**	Trust based on the observation that other team members actively include me in their social and work activities
10.	**Accessibility**	Trust based on the observation that other team members share their true feelings and I can relate to them on a personal level

Our work has confirmed that these ten criteria for trust can be used to provide a working definition of trust relevant in emergency-response situations. They can then be divided into two categories: swift trust and deeper trust.

Swift trust	Deeper trust
Competence Openness with information Integrity Reciprocity	Compatibility Goodwill Predictability Well-being Inclusion Accessibility
Swift trust can be more readily achieved and is necessary from early stages of emergency response.	**Deeper trust takes more time to establish and requires focused effort on an ongoing basis throughout the emergency response.**

On the basis of the research findings, a number of 'tools' for measuring and building trust within emergency-response teams have been developed (see Section 4). Together they provide a toolkit for teams and their leaders to manage the levels of trust within the team and promote the benefits that come from high levels of trust between team members. Just as the financial implications of all actions and decisions need to be taken into account, so also do the trust implications. Will certain actions or decisions add to or reduce the stock of trust within the team?

Trust within the team is, of course, only the starting point. Trust between the team and the local community, between different agencies and with the funding bodies, are also of crucial importance. But without trust within the team, communication and delivery will be patchy and un-co-ordinated, and trust between the team and the rest of the world will be damaged.

The section below gives more detail on the ten criteria that influence levels of trust in teams. Throughout this toolkit the criteria for trust will be referenced in order to anchor the tools within an accessible and field-tested framework that aims to build trust in teams.

The ten criteria for trust

Swift trust

Competence

Trust based on a perception that team members are competent, and so will not let me down.

Every day we have to trust people. When we go to the doctor and take her advice we trust that she is a competent doctor and understands things that we do not. When we fly on an aeroplane we trust that the pilot who flies it and the engineers who have serviced it know what they are doing and will do a good job. We trust them because we believe they are competent at their jobs. In the same way, in the emergency-response team we need to trust that other people in the team are competent at their jobs and will perform to a good standard. If this is not the case then other team members cannot do their job properly; frustrations will increase and trust will diminish.

Openness with information

Trust based on the observation that other team members share information important to the team proactively and clearly.

Information is power. Those who have access to information and do not share it with others are creating a power differential. On one hand, if we believe that other people have information that is important for us and they are not sharing it with us we may become suspicious. We may begin to wonder what the information is, and why they are not sharing it. This suspicion breeds mistrust. On the other hand, when someone does share information with us, it sends a positive signal that they do trust us. We are more likely to feel trusting towards them. Sometimes, it is necessary to keep information confidential for good reasons. In such cases, the team must understand the reasons. Sometimes, how we share information can be conditioned by our cultural background. In certain cultures people learn to be more direct and task-focused with people they don't know well. In other cultures people tend only to be clear and proactive in sharing information with those they have developed a personal relationship with.

Integrity

Trust based on the observation that other team members maintain promises, are team-orientated, and behave towards me in accordance with a moral code.

If people keep their word and fulfill their commitments, over time, we come to trust them more. It is sometimes tempting to promise things that we are not sure we can deliver, just to please people. This tends to be the case in certain cultural contexts where saying 'no' might be regarded as bad for relationships. In the long run, when we cannot deliver, this reduces other people's trust in us. It takes time to build trust. We need to see that the other person is consistent in keeping their word. On occasion, we may not be able to keep to our commitments for reasons outside our control. When this happens, it is important that we explain the circumstances to the people we have made a commitment to.

Another aspect of integrity is behaving in accordance with our professed moral codes and standards. The quickest way to breed cynicism and destroy trust is to commend one form of behaviour and then not to live by that standard oneself.

Finally, integrity sometimes requires us to put the interests of the team and other team members above our own personal interests. When others see this behaviour, they understand that we are prepared to make sacrifices in the interests of the common good. This will increase trust.

Reciprocity

Trust based on the observation that other team members are trusting and co-operative towards me.

It is easier to trust someone else if we feel they are trusting towards us. Equally, if we feel someone is behaving towards us in a suspicious way, then we can easily project negative motivations onto them in order to explain their behaviour, and this makes it more difficult for us to trust them. This reciprocal nature of trust means that we can quickly get into positive or negative 'spirals' of trust. If I behave in a way that sends out a message of trust to others, then typically they will see this and reciprocate with some trust-building behaviours themselves. So small behaviours that show trust can lead to larger, more significant trust behaviours and a positive 'spiral' is created. But to start this positive cycle we may have to take some personal risks and make ourselves vulnerable in some way. Of course, it is also possible to create a negative cycle and to destroy trust very quickly by a careless word or action. This negative cycle can be made worse by cultural misunderstandings. Direct, open feedback can sometimes be seen as aggression and an indirect, face-saving style can be seen as hiding something.

Deeper trust

Compatibility

Trust based on background, values, approaches, interests, and objectives held in common.

Most of us feel more comfortable and more ready to trust in the company of people who are 'like us'. In reality, we are all different from each other. We are different in terms of, for example, personalities, experience, gender, and culture. We have to understand and work through these differences before we cease to notice them and feel instead that we are all part of something bigger and more important than ourselves. To build trust in the culturally diverse context of emergency-response teams, we need to create and articulate common objectives that we can all commit to; we need to establish ways of working and communicating with each other that utilise the best resources of the team; and, we need to find, share, and understand common interests, values, and beliefs. If the things that unite us are emphasised, the things that make us different will become less noticeable and less of a barrier.

Goodwill

Trust based on the belief that other team members are concerned about my overall welfare.

Working in an emergency-response team is a demanding and stressful experience. No-one is immune from these pressures and everyone needs help and support from time to time. If I feel that other people in the team are concerned about me and how I am feeling, I can trust them more easily. At one level there are the simple needs – food, rest, and shelter, often in difficult circumstances. But at a more fundamental level I need to know that others in the team are concerned about me as an individual. Do they notice and comfort me when I am tired or depressed? Do they recognise that I have a family and friends outside the context of the emergency? Do they take the time to get to know me and understand the things that are important for me? Do they openly value the contribution I am trying to make to the overall effort? If I believe that they do, then I will find it easier to trust them. Of course if I take the initiative to look out for other team members then they are more likely to do the same for me. I may need to remember, however, that 'goodwill' may be a stronger criterion for trusting others in cultures where personal relationships are a pre-requisite for trust.

Predictability

Trust based on the observation that the behaviour of team members is consistent over time and in different contexts.

Trusting others involves taking a risk about their future behaviour. If I trust someone enough to lend them some money, I am taking the risk that they may not pay me back. To trust a stranger in this way is usually unwise, because I have no way of predicting their behaviour from a knowledge of their past actions. On the other hand if I lend some money to a good friend then I can form a view about the level of risk involved from her/his behaviour in the past. To reduce the risks associated with trusting, therefore, I need to be able to see consistent patterns of behaviour. People who behave in erratic and unpredictable ways are not so trustworthy because I cannot identify the patterns and so I do not know how they will behave in this particular instance. On the other hand, I will find it easier to trust people who are disciplined in their approach to work and abide by the norms and standards of the group in their everyday lives, as these qualities make their behaviour more predictable. Sometimes I may lose trust in those from other cultural backgrounds because they may behave in ways that seem unpredictable, as I don't fully understand the values that lie behind their actions, and how they may differ from my own. It is essential therefore to increase understanding of our own and other people's different cultural tendencies.

Well-being

Trust arising from the feeling that I have nothing to fear from other members of the team.

It is difficult to fear and trust people at the same time. Sometimes fear of an outside threat can lead us to trust the people in our own group more strongly, as often happens in times of war or heightened security threats. But we are not likely to find it easy to trust the people who make us afraid. In the working environment the most common cause of fear is a culture of 'blame'. When something goes wrong, then first reactions are to look for the person whose 'fault' it was with a view to punishing them. Such a culture destroys trust and leads people to behave in a defensive way – thinking always about how they can justify their actions if necessary; this in turn leads to less communication, less initiative-taking, and less innovation. A sure sign of a 'blame' culture and low levels of trust is when people start asking for everything in writing.

Inclusion

Trust based on the observation that other team members actively include me in their social and work activities.

Some people are more sociable than others. They enjoy being with a group. Some people are more comfortable with one or two other people at a time. Nevertheless, all of us need to be included in important social and work activities. Excluding someone, leaving them out of activities that involve everyone else, sends a powerful message that destroys trust. In the context of an emergency-response team there is always a danger that factions or sub-groups will form. These may be based on whether some people are 'internationals' and some 'nationals'. Sub-groups may also form based on ethnic differences or simply on the basis of functional or regional separation. To some extent these divisions are inevitable and even natural. For example, it is important to remember that some people may need to spend time with others who share their mother tongue, especially when they are living and working in difficult situations and using another language in their work with the team. However, if these groupings become too strong, and especially if members of an 'in-group' hold a lot of power within the team, the feelings of those who are excluded can quickly lower levels of trust. Careful thought must be given to such things as who should be invited to meetings, who should be included in communications, and who should be involved in social events. These decisions send out powerful messages of trust or mistrust.

Accessibility

Trust based on the observation that other team members share their true feelings and I can relate to them on a personal level.

People who are cool and distant in their personal manner may seem more difficult to trust. By keeping their thoughts and feelings to themselves they seem to be indicating that they do not trust others and are not prepared to take the risk of making themselves vulnerable. Other people, who are open with their emotions and express their wishes and needs in a sincere way, may seem to be demonstrating trust in the people around them and so may more readily invoke trusting behaviours in response (see Reciprocity above). Accessibility may be a stronger criterion for trusting others in cultures that place more emphasis on open expression of emotions than others.

2 • The Trust Index

How to measure factors that impact on trust in teams

A key conclusion of the Building Trust Project research into the role of trust in emergency-response situations was that, although trust was considered essential for the effective operation of diverse teams, there were at the time no explicit ways of measuring it. One part of the structured interview used in this research addressed the question of how a culture of trust could be measured. The most common response was that the best indicator of trust is the performance and output of the team. In other words, if the team is achieving its objectives and performing well then there must be trust present. This response helps to cement the view that there is a clear link between trust and performance, but does not really help with measuring trust. If we believe that trust is first in the causal relationship (i.e. good levels of trust result in good outputs), then we need to find more specific ways of measuring trust itself. While team leaders and their reports were sensitive to observable symptoms of high and low levels of trust from their considerable experience in the field, they had no specific ways of assessing trust factors as a platform for focused emergency work.

There are two ways of assessing trust in teams – indirect and direct. The indirect method relies on measuring and assessing the factors that are likely to affect trust levels within the team. The direct method relies on observing the behaviours of team members and/or asking for their views through interviews or questionnaires. The tool that was developed out of the research – the Trust Index – is an example of an indirect method of describing trust. It has been developed because the original research revealed some key factors – linked to the composition, leadership, and alignment of the team and the environmental, organisational, and cultural context in which a team operates – that clearly inhibited or promoted levels of trust within the team in an emergency-response situation. These factors consisted of more than simply the behaviours of team members, but they had an enormous *impact* on trust behaviours developed within the team. It was felt that by identifying, understanding, and responding to specific factors that cause a lower level of trust in a team, the team would then be in the best position to actively manage trust levels in the team.

Guidance notes

What is the Index used for?

The Trust Index has been developed as a way of assessing the factors that enhance or destroy trust within emergency-response teams. It provides a framework for the team leaders and team members to actively manage the levels of trust within the team. It does not seek to measure trust levels directly, but indirectly, by looking at the factors that impact on the level of trust within the team. The objective of the Index is to raise levels of awareness within the emergency-response team about trust, and to form the basis of discussions and an action plan on how trust within the team can be enhanced and maintained.

Why use the Index?

Creating a culture of trust in an emergency-response team needs to become a central objective for the leader and all members of the team. Research and experience shows that where this can be achieved, the effectiveness of the team in delivering benefits to the community will be substantially enhanced. Without identifying and understanding specific factors that are influencing levels of trust in a team, it is difficult for a leader to build trust.

What does the Index consist of?

The Trust Index (page 22) is divided into six types of factors affecting trust:

- **Environmental factors:** relating to elements in the community and the general environment in which the team is operating.
- **Organisational factors:** relating to the structures, systems, and procedures needed to ensure that staff are properly supported, and that uncertainty about working arrangements is reduced to a minimum.
- **Leadership factors:** relating to the qualities and style of the team leader.
- **Team-composition factors:** relating to the make-up of the team including skills, experience, styles, gender, personality etc.
- **Alignment factors:** relating to arrangements to ensure that personal relationships and a shared sense of purpose are developed within the team, including the management of cultural differences.
- **Cultural factors:** relating to the cultural dimension of team interactions.

Within each of these types there are a number of specific factors, each with a –5 to +5 scale. At the right-hand end of the scale is a brief description of the situation that is likely to enhance trust. At the left-hand end of the scale is a description of the corresponding situation that inhibits the promotion of trust.

Any score above 0 would indicate that this factor is enhancing trust. The positive score reflects the extent to which team members feel it is, in practice, enhancing trust. A score of +5 on a given factor means that it is enhancing trust to a high degree, and the team does not need to focus on further improvement. Any score below 0 would indicate that this factor is diminishing or destroying trust, and the negative score reflects the extent to which team members feel it is destroying trust. A score of –5 on a given factor means that it is a major factor in destroying trust within the team. A score of 0 can be used to indicate a factor that is neutral. It means that, at the moment, this factor is not impacting on the level of trust in the team.

Who is the Index for?

Groups working with a shared aim, mutual dependency, and common leadership can use the Index. Because the Trust Index is designed for diverse teams responding to emergencies, it will have the highest relevance to those teams. Therefore, it is important that the Index is used by the entire team, including the team leader, international agency staff, local agency staff, and new local recruits. The Trust Index may also be useful in a wide range of team contexts falling under the umbrella of emergency relief. These may include:

- a water/sanitation team operating in a particular field site;
- a team of programme co-ordinators at that field site who all report to the same person (i.e. the field co-ordinator or deputy director of programmes);
- a finance team at the main office;
- a senior-management team at the main office who all report to the same person (i.e. the country director).

When to use the Index

The Trust Index should be used, and each of the scales rated, as soon as possible after an emergency has been declared, but after the team members have had some experience of each other and of the style/approach of the team leader. It should then be used every three months thereafter in order to track team progress. As it is the first step of an ongoing process, and as issues may be raised regarding organisational procedures, it should be used when there is commitment from the country director and senior-management team to address the issues raised during the process. It will also take a commitment from the team itself to create and follow a specific work plan to improve levels of trust where gaps have been identified.

How long does the Index take to complete?

Completing the Trust Index process will take approximately three hours, distributed over the first seven stages described below in 'How to use the Index'.

Who leads the process?

The person who leads the process of introducing and completing the Trust Index can be a team leader or an external facilitator (either from inside or outside the agency). The advantage of the team leader leading the process is that team leaders can build motivation and trust by modelling a spirit of openness and transparency in leadership style. From a practical perspective team leaders can more flexibly mould the process around regular team meetings.

The advantage of an external facilitator leading the process is that the team leader will be freed up to participate in the discussion without at the same time having to lead the process. External facilitators with cultural awareness can also help to encourage participation in those cultural contexts where discussing leadership issues in the presence of your team leader may be uncommon or uncomfortable.

How to use the Index

The first time that the Index is used, particularly in the initial response phase of an emergency-response situation, it is recommended to go through the following eight stages:

1. The team leader/facilitator, working with a senior local stakeholder (a long-term local staff member and/or someone with an in-depth understanding of the local operating environment), completes the 'Environmental factors' section of the Trust Index before meeting the team.

   Approximate time for stage 1: 20 minutes.

2. The team leader/facilitator introduces the Index at a team meeting, putting a strong focus on the importance of a culture of trust in emergency-response teams. The challenge of working under pressure in highly diverse groups and the importance of making higher levels of trust a shared team objective are emphasised in the introduction. Using this tool is a way of identifying potential gaps in building a culture of trust, before working to close them. If the team leader/facilitator needs a common understanding of what is meant by 'trust', a simple brainstorming exercise can be run, where the group is asked to think through their past experiences of how it felt to be in a team with high trust and a team with low trust. They can then put themselves in the position of a 'Trust Doctor', listing the symptoms of each.

3. The team leader/facilitator begins by introducing the 'Environmental factors' and discussing the results with the team. The team leader/facilitator should then use their best judgement about how to introduce the rest of the Index to the team. Either give out copies of the entire Index, or break it down into its constituent parts and give out each of the sections separately (to allow team members to take it in slowly). The team leader/facilitator explains that each team member will rate each of the factors in the five other sections in the Index (organisational, leadership, team composition, alignment, and cultural) in a similar way, using the scales provided. The team leader/ facilitator provides a short description of each section and gives an example of how to use the scale with one item from the Index. To ensure that there is a clearly defined and shared focus among team members in completing the Index, a clear reminder must be given as to who exactly they are considering as the 'team' and who the team leader is. They must also be told when completing the Index to consider where the team is now, and not reflect on past issues. They should also be told that their responses will be anonymous, and that the process is most valuable when team members can be as open as possible about their opinions.

   Approximate time for stages 2 & 3: 20 minutes.

4. The team leader/facilitator should ensure that everyone completes the Index and hands it in before they leave this first meeting, if possible (without writing their names on their copies, in order to keep their ratings anonymous). Alternatively, a deadline can be given for the completion and return of the Index before the next team meeting, and each individual team member (including the leader) makes the time before the deadline to complete their own individual assessments based on their experience and perceptions. These ratings should be made anonymously and the completed copies of the Index should be sent to a central location in sealed envelopes to ensure confidentiality. Note that the team leader should not complete the section on leadership.

   Approximate time for stage 4: 20 minutes.

(NB A second option for completing the Index would be to do this in a room together on the same day, and with time dedicated to complete and review results section by section. Individuals can complete the Index on their own, or in order to encourage participation, the Index can be completed in pairs, with two people sitting together and coming to a consensus about what score to assign. This option will take longer.)

5. There are two alternatives for scoring the Index. The first option is that the team leader or a nominated team member/external facilitator could average the ratings of all team members for each factor. This will provide specific 'scores' for each factor. In this way the strongest and weakest areas within a particular section can be identified. The factors can then also be averaged together for each section (see the first example in Handout A: Example Scoring Sheets). The result will be a completed 'Trust Index' for each of the factors, which will be distributed and discussed by the whole team at the next meeting.

    While averages are easier to process, and they protect individuals more, the perspective of the range/spread of answers is lost. It can be illuminating to see the variety of opinions from within a team regarding a particular factor. Therefore, a second option is to map out a detailed breakdown of the responses for each section on a flip-chart, making areas of differing opinion clearly visible (see the second example in Handout A: Example Scoring Sheets). Factors with a wider spread of answers can then be discussed. This often leads to more in-depth and lively examination of a particular factor. This is also a useful technique for more visual learners.

    Approximate time for stage 5: 30 minutes.

6. The team leader/facilitator distributes the overall trust scores and facilitates a team discussion. The final objective of this discussion is to identify things to be done to build trust. To set the discussion in a positive context, it is worth discussing which factors in each section are optimising trust within the team and why, before going on to look at the lower scores. The meeting needs to be open and participative. It should be managed in such a way that everyone has an equal opportunity to share their ideas and views. This may involve dividing into pairs or small groups to discuss the reason for lower scores and then feeding the results of the discussion back in a joint session all together.

    Approximate time for stage 6: 60 minutes.

7. The team needs to develop a Trust Index Action Plan (see Handout B: Trust Index Action Plan) which should:

    •   identify factors that need to be improved;

    •   identify activities to ensure that those factors that are reducing and destroying trust in the team are actively managed.

    The team should also discuss what needs to be done to ensure that those factors that are optimising trust in the team are nurtured and supported throughout the team life-cycle.

    Approximate time for stage 7: 30 minutes

8. The Trust Index should be completed again, if possible, three months later, to monitor how trust in the team is developing, and the impact of the changes made.

(NB The important thing for the team to focus on is not the absolute level of the Index but its movement over time. In some situations there will be factors that make the creation of high levels of trust within the team difficult. In such cases, the scores will initially be low, which may mean that focused effort and attention is required to create good levels of trust. In other situations the starting point will be higher and it will be easier to create trust. In either case the objective of the process should be to consider the trust implications of actions and decisions, and to ensure that over time the levels of trust grow.)

What do I need to remember when deciding to use the Index?

1. Deciding to use the Index conveys an important message that trust is taken seriously as a key factor in impacting emergency response. The very process of carrying out this exercise can lead to increasing trust within the team.

2. Carrying out this exercise might also lead to tense discussions and high expectations that problems will be quickly resolved.

3. Genuine commitment from leadership to follow through is important, as well as team commitment to work on the issues identified.

4. If tensions within the team do arise over particular factors in the Index, and are beyond the skills of the leader or facilitator to resolve, the leader or facilitator should seek advice from appropriate sources such as the local human-resources manager, the head-office human-resources focal point, or the appropriate learning and development adviser who can offer targeted and structured support to the team leader and team members.

Handout A: Example Scoring Sheets for the Trust Index

Example scoring sheet 1

This scoring sheet is an example of the first scoring method outlined in step 5 of 'How to use the Index'. The method identifies average team scores for each section of the Index.

First collect each team member's completed Index. Beginning with the Organisational factors, take the first factor, add up each team member's score for that factor, and divide the sum by the number of team members scoring that factor. This will give you the average, which should be written in the table.

Proceed in the same way for each of the Organisational factors. The team may want to discuss why some average scores within the Organisational factors column are higher or lower than others. Now add up all of the average scores in the Organisational column and insert the sum in the Total score box.

Divide the sum by the total number of factors (13 for this section) and insert the number in the Average box.

Follow the same pattern for each of the other Index sections. If desired, each column's total score can be added together and the sum can be divided by five (total number of columns) to come up with an Overall average

Factor	Section of the Index						
	Organisational	**Leadership**	**Team composition**	**Alignment**	**Cultural**		
1	2.3	2.1	2	1.5	1.4		
2	2.5	3	3.1	2.4	1.3		
3	3.5	4	2.4	3.6	1.9		
4	1	2.1	1.7	2	2.2		
5	-0.3	3	2.5	-1			
6	2.1	2.2	3.2	-2			
7	3.1	3.3	2.6	-1.4			
8	4	2.3		1.8			
9	2			2.1			
10	1			2.2			
11	1			3.3			
12	2			2.6			
13	2.2						
Total score	26.4	22	17.5	17.1	6.8		**Overall average**
Average	2	2.8	2.5	1.4	1.7		2.1

This chart can be used each time the team completes the Index, and the team can discuss any differences between previous and current scores (for each section, factor, and the overall score).

Handout A: Example Scoring Sheets for the Trust Index

Example scoring sheet 2

This scoring sheet provides a visual representation of scores on a flip-chart. It shows the spread of scores and avoids a specific numeric score. The team leader/facilitator can use this method of scoring the Index if the team is comprised of more visual learners, if a numeric score is not desired, or if time is short.

Simply draw a grid on flip-chart paper with the rows representing each factor in a section (13 rows for the Organisational section, for example) and the columns representing the score (-5 to +5).

Make one mark in a box for each team member's score. On the flip-chart below that was prepared for the Alignment section, three staff marked a '4' for factor 4, and two staff marked a '5'.

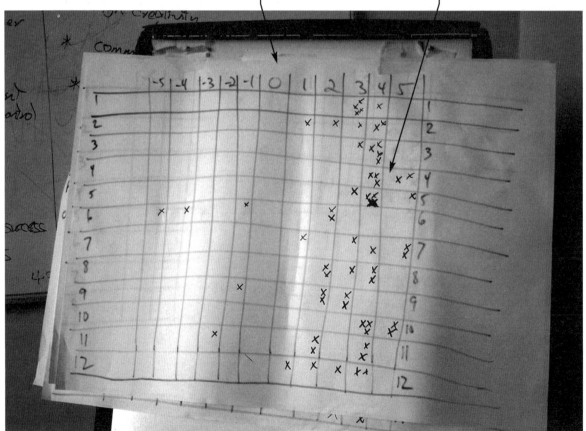

Amy Bess/ECB Project, Oxfam GB

In this example, the team leader/facilitator may want to lead a discussion about why factor 4 was ranked so highly and why there was a wider spread of scores for factor 6.

Handout B: Trust Index Action Plan

Date	
Location	
Team	

FACTORS	1 Strength of factor (Index score)	2 Factor elements to improve (top two priorities)	3 Activities to support improvement of priority elements	4 Expected activity completion date	5 Responsible team members
Environmental					
Organisational					
Leadership					
Team compostion					
Alignment					
Cultural					

Team leader	
Senior local stakeholder/team member	
Date for review of the plan	

Instructions

Complete the Trust Index with the team. Average the scores for each factor and enter into column one. Discuss the score and relative importance of the elements for each factor. Select the top two factors that are critical to strengthening, and that the team has the ability to influence. Enter these into column two. Discuss with the team what kinds of activities or action will be taken to strengthen these two factors. Enter the activities into column three. Decide when the activities will be accomplished and enter the dates into column four. Discuss who in the team needs to take action to ensure that the activities are accomplished. Enter the names into column five. Set a date for a review of the action plan.

The Trust Index tool

Trust Index: environmental factors

These factors which affect trust in emergency-response teams relate to elements in the community and the general environment in which the team is operating. The team will not be able to change these factors by their own actions, but may be able to mitigate any negative impact on trust levels within the team.

	Makes trust in response teams more difficult											Makes trust in response teams easier
1	The community is complex and divided, possibly with hostilities between different ethnic, religious, or other groups	-5	-4	-3	-2	-1	0	1	2	3	4	5	The community is well-integrated with a legitimate government and good governance
2	The response to the emergency is likely to create or increase divisions within the community	-5	-4	-3	-2	-1	0	1	2	3	4	5	The response to the emergency is likely to unite the community behind a common effort
3	The government and/or the agency has little or no experience of this type of emergency in this country or geographical area	-5	-4	-3	-2	-1	0	1	2	3	4	5	The government and/or the agency has extensive experience of dealing with this type of emergency in this country or geographical area
4	Humanitarian agencies are in a competitive relationship with each other and there is no effective co-ordination	-5	-4	-3	-2	-1	0	1	2	3	4	5	There is an organisation (e.g. national or local government, NGO, or the UN) providing effective inter-agency co-ordination
5	International and/or external involvement is resented by the local government and the local community	-5	-4	-3	-2	-1	0	1	2	3	4	5	International and/or external involvement is welcomed by the local government and the local community
6	The local population from which to recruit is inexperienced and people have few relevant technical skills	-5	-4	-3	-2	-1	0	1	2	3	4	5	The local population from which to recruit is highly experienced and people have good technical skills
7	The geographical spread of the emergency makes communications more difficult within the widespread team and between the team and regional and/or head office	-5	-4	-3	-2	-1	0	1	2	3	4	5	The geographical location of the emergency allows emergency-team members to remain together in one area, with easy communications with regional and/or head office

Trust Index: organisational factors

Trust Index: organisational factors

These factors which affect trust in emergency-response teams relate to the structures, systems, and procedures needed to ensure that staff are properly supported and uncertainty about working arrangements is reduced to a minimum.

	Makes trust in response teams more difficult											Makes trust in response teams easier
1	This agency did not have a national office in this affected country prior to the emergency	-5	-4	-3	-2	-1	0	1	2	3	4	5	The established national office in the affected country provides systems and process support
2	There is no organigram in place, and roles and responsibilities are not clear	-5	-4	-3	-2	-1	0	1	2	3	4	5	There is an organigram in place, and roles and responsibilities are clearly defined by job descriptions
3	There are no performance measures or feedback processes, or those that exist are not in use	-5	-4	-3	-2	-1	0	1	2	3	4	5	Personal and team performance measures and feedback processes are in place and in use for all staff
4	There are no systematic arrangements for identifying or meeting staff skills gaps	-5	-4	-3	-2	-1	0	1	2	3	4	5	Staff skills gaps are identified and are being met with appropriate training and development programmes
5	There are no clear systems of delegated authority and accountability, or those that are in place are perceived as unfair and inefficient	-5	-4	-3	-2	-1	0	1	2	3	4	5	There are clear and efficient systems in place for delegating authority and assuring accountability, and they are perceived as fair and appropriate
6	There are no effective communication systems or easy ways to access information within the organisation	-5	-4	-3	-2	-1	0	1	2	3	4	5	There are effective communication systems and easy ways to access information within the organisation
7	No team meetings are held	-5	-4	-3	-2	-1	0	1	2	3	4	5	There are regular and documented team meetings taking place (face-to-face or virtually)

Trust Index: organisational factors   continued

These factors which affect trust in emergency-response teams relate to the structures, systems, and procedures needed to ensure that staff are properly supported and uncertainty about working arrangements is reduced to a minimum.

	Makes trust in response teams more difficult	-5	-4	-3	-2	-1	0	1	2	3	4	5	Makes trust in response teams easier
8	Differentials of salaries and benefits between team members are not understood or are perceived as unfair or inappropriate	-5	-4	-3	-2	-1	0	1	2	3	4	5	Differentials of salaries and benefits between team members are understood and perceived as fair and appropriate
9	Decisions are not taken	-5	-4	-3	-2	-1	0	1	2	3	4	5	Effective processes are in place so that decisions are taken, communicated to team members with explanations where necessary, and implemented quickly
10	Team members are unaware of what work they should be doing and how their work fits into a wider plan	-5	-4	-3	-2	-1	0	1	2	3	4	5	Team members are clear about what work they should be doing and how their work fits into a wider plan
11	National/local staff are not involved in hiring decisions and procedures	-5	-4	-3	-2	-1	0	1	2	3	4	5	National/local staff are involved in hiring decisions and procedures
12	The well-being of staff is not considered	-5	-4	-3	-2	-1	0	1	2	3	4	5	The well-being of staff is looked after: adequate time off is ensured; stress-awareness materials are provided and discussed; psycho-social support is provided when needed
13	Security procedures are not in place or not enforced	-5	-4	-3	-2	-1	0	1	2	3	4	5	Effective security procedures are in place and are enforced

Trust Index: leadership factors

These factors which affect trust in emergency-response teams relate to the qualities and style of the team leader(s).

	Makes trust in response teams more difficult	-5	-4	-3	-2	-1	0	1	2	3	4	5	Makes trust in response teams easier
1	Team leader(s) have little local/regional knowledge or experience and do not use the services of acknowledged local resource persons	-5	-4	-3	-2	-1	0	1	2	3	4	5	Team leader(s) have a high level of local/regional knowledge and experience and/or have identified and use the services of acknowledged local resource persons
2	Team leader(s) do not seem influential within the organisation and are not able to get approvals from regional or head office	-5	-4	-3	-2	-1	0	1	2	3	4	5	Team leader(s) are well-networked and influential within the organisation and are able to get approvals from regional or head office
3	Team leader(s) are not culturally sensitive and have no previous experience of working with multi-cultural or diverse teams	-5	-4	-3	-2	-1	0	1	2	3	4	5	Team leader(s) are culturally sensitive and effective in leading diverse teams
4	Team leader(s) provide little structure or guidance and leave people to find their own way	-5	-4	-3	-2	-1	0	1	2	3	4	5	Team leader(s) create a predictable and well-organised environment for the team to work in
5	Team leader(s) behave in a way that does not support organisational values and ethics	-5	-4	-3	-2	-1	0	1	2	3	4	5	Team leader(s) behave in a way that supports organisational values and ethics
6	Team leader(s) do not communicate well with team members	-5	-4	-3	-2	-1	0	1	2	3	4	5	Team leader(s) communicate freely with all team members and make clear what they expect from the team
7	Team leader(s) try to do everything themselves and do not delegate	-5	-4	-3	-2	-1	0	1	2	3	4	5	Team leader(s) delegate tasks and share responsibility and authority
8	Team leader(s) make all decisions without consulting with team members	-5	-4	-3	-2	-1	0	1	2	3	4	5	Team leader(s) seek and listen to the ideas and opinions of team members and involve the team in decision-making

Trust Index: team-composition factors

	These factors which affect trust in emergency-response teams relate to the make-up of the team.											
	Makes trust in response teams more difficult											**Makes trust in response teams easier**
1	Many posts are filled with recruits who are not qualified	-5	-4	-3	-2	-1	0	1	2	3	4	5	All posts are filled with people who have the appropriate skills and experience (or appropriate capacity-building and training is under way)
2	The diversity of team members in terms of culture, religion, gender, age, and ethnic group is not recognised or valued as an advantage	-5	-4	-3	-2	-1	0	1	2	3	4	5	The diversity of team members in terms of culture, religion, gender, age, and ethnic group is recognised as an advantage, and efforts to diversify are actively pursued
3	The team is unable to effectively communicate and address substantial differences in languages and culture-based communication styles	-5	-4	-3	-2	-1	0	1	2	3	4	5	The team members identify and address any differences in language and communication styles and are able to communicate effectively
4	The team is comprised of people with a limited range of skills and work styles	-5	-4	-3	-2	-1	0	1	2	3	4	5	The team is comprised of people with a range of different skills and work styles
5	Team members are not open with each other, and lack awareness and skills to work with people from different cultures	-5	-4	-3	-2	-1	0	1	2	3	4	5	Team members are open, respectful, self-aware, and capable of working with people from different cultures
6	Aside from the team leader, power is not balanced amongst team members; power is held by a few individuals or 'in-groups' (based on gender, nationality, etc.)	-5	-4	-3	-2	-1	0	1	2	3	4	5	Aside from the team leader, power is perceived to be balanced and distributed amongst the team members
7	No efforts are made to assure a gender and diversity balance within the team	-5	-4	-3	-2	-1	0	1	2	3	4	5	Gender and diversity balance is actively pursued through recruitment into the team, and capacity-building is in place to ensure all staff are able to contribute effectively to the work of the team

Building Trust in Diverse Teams

Trust Index: alignment factors

These factors which affect trust in emergency-response teams relate to arrangements to ensure that personal relationships and a shared sense of purpose are developed within the team

	Makes trust in response teams more difficult	-5	-4	-3	-2	-1	0	1	2	3	4	5	Makes trust in response teams easier
1	Team members lack knowledge of and commitment to organisational values	-5	-4	-3	-2	-1	0	1	2	3	4	5	All team members can articulate and demonstrate an understanding and acceptance of organisational values
2	Team members are confused about the team's purpose and responsibilities	-5	-4	-3	-2	-1	0	1	2	3	4	5	The team's purpose or main objectives are well-understood by all team members, and each team member's role and responsibilities are clearly defined and understood by every other member of the team
3	Key team processes have not been discussed or agreed, and team members do not have a common understanding of these issues	-5	-4	-3	-2	-1	0	1	2	3	4	5	Team members are involved in discussing and agreeing key team processes (e.g. how meetings should be conducted and how conflicts should be resolved)
4	There is no common understanding about what behaviours are acceptable or unacceptable within the context of the team	-5	-4	-3	-2	-1	0	1	2	3	4	5	Behaviours that are acceptable and unacceptable for team members have been identified, discussed, and agreed within the team
5	No social activities for team members take place to help all staff build relationships	-5	-4	-3	-2	-1	0	1	2	3	4	5	Social activities involving all team members are organised on a regular basis to help all staff build relationships
6	Team successes are not recognised in any way	-5	-4	-3	-2	-1	0	1	2	3	4	5	Team successes are recognised and celebrated

Trust Index: alignment factors

continued

These factors which affect trust in emergency-response teams relate to arrangements to ensure that personal relationships and a shared sense of purpose are developed within the team

	Makes trust in response teams more difficult	-5	-4	-3	-2	-1	0	1	2	3	4	5	**Makes trust in response teams easier**
7	The team does not reflect on its performance	-5	-4	-3	-2	-1	0	1	2	3	4	5	Team sessions are held where team performance is reviewed and improvements made as needed
8	Team gatherings/communications only focus on immediate task issues	-5	-4	-3	-2	-1	0	1	2	3	4	5	Team gatherings/communications go beyond a focus on immediate tasks to develop and update a shared sense of purpose
9	There is no shared understanding about what, where, when, and how communication between team members should take place	-5	-4	-3	-2	-1	0	1	2	3	4	5	An agreed communication charter or equivalent is in place and there is shared understanding about what should be communicated, by when, and by whom
10	There is little understanding within the team about the overall purpose and mission of the organisation; knowledge is limited to immediate activities	-5	-4	-3	-2	-1	0	1	2	3	4	5	There is good understanding within the team about the overall purpose and mission of the organisation
11	There are high levels of staff turnover in the team (including team leaders)	-5	-4	-3	-2	-1	0	1	2	3	4	5	The team is stable, with low levels of staff turnover (including team leaders)
12	There is no orientation for new team members	-5	-4	-3	-2	-1	0	1	2	3	4	5	New team members participate in a comprehensive orientation and are smoothly integrated into the team

Trust Index: cultural factors

The statements about particular cultural groups in the following four sections on cultural differences refer to tendencies within cultures; it should be remembered that each individual person is unique and will undoubtedly bring their own personal experiences, values, and approaches into any context.

Communication style

How do cultural differences in communication style impact on your team? When communicating, all of us need to decide whether to focus on text (the explicit and direct use of words) or context (what is between the lines or non-verbal). Team members from more 'low-context' (high 'text') cultures tend to learn from their national cultural background that effective communication is about 'saying what you mean and meaning what you say'. They tend to rely on written communication (e.g. minutes of meetings, agendas, contracts) to 'spell out' meaning. Trust is built quickly by being clear and focusing on the task. North Americans, Australasians, and Northern Europeans tend to be brought up to have a low-context approach to communication.

Team members from more 'high-context' (low 'text') cultures tend to learn from their national cultural background to value the ability of the sensitive listener who can 'read between the lines', and understand the damage done to relationships by direct talking. They tend to avoid writing and rely on broad spoken agreements. Trust is built slowly by 'saving face', i.e. protecting oneself from public humiliation and/or embarrassment and focusing on relationship. South and South-East Asians, Africans, Middle-Easterners, and South Europeans tend to have a high-context approach.

Look at the following behaviours and beliefs connected to low- and high-context work environments, and consider whether you have such cultural differences in your team.

Low-context	High-context
Be direct and task-focused	Be indirect and relationship-focused
Be explicit and specific	Communicate between the lines or though non-verbal means
Write things down and 'spell things out'	Keep things oral
Give feedback as soon as possible, in a direct manner	Give feedback indirectly, and at the right time in order to save face
Believe that trust in your competence leads to deeper levels of relationships, so begin with the task	Believe that deeper levels of personal trust are required for tasks to be carried out effectively, so begin with relationship-building
Believe that being clear shows respect	Believe that sensitivity about saving face shows respect

A combination of both low-context and high-context cultural preferences can lead to great synergies in nurturing trust in international teams where trust is fragile. Combining 'clarity' (low-context) with 'rapport' (high-context) is critical for building a productive working atmosphere. However, when these differences are not recognised and respected, the result can be the opposite. Low-context directness can be perceived as 'insensitivity' and high-context indirectness can be considered as 'time-wasting'.

How are these differences handled in your team? Are they ignored and not respected, leading to misunderstandings and mis-evaluations? Or are they openly recognised and reconciled so that trust is built? If you are working in a fairly mono-cultural team and such differences are irrelevant, score '0'.

Makes trust in response teams more difficult											Makes trust in response teams easier
This difference is not recognised, discussed, or respected, leading to misunderstandings and mis-evaluations	-5	-4	-3	-2	-1	0	1	2	3	4	5	This difference is recognised, discussed, and respected, so that trust is built

Power and equality

How do cultural differences in attitudes to power and equality impact on your team? Team members from 'low power-distance' cultures tend to learn to expect and accept that gaps in power and social status between them and their bosses should be minimised. They tend to expect to be consulted by their bosses, who empower them in return for initiative. North Americans, Australasians, and Northern Europeans tend to be brought up to have a low power-distance approach.

Team members from 'high power-distance' cultures tend to learn to expect and accept a large gap in power and social status between them and their bosses. They tend to have more dependent relationships with strong, decisive, and often paternalistic bosses who provide security in return for loyalty. South and South-East Asians, Africans, Middle-Easterners, South Americans, as well as Southern Europeans tend to have a high power-distance approach.

Look at the following behaviours and beliefs connected to low and high power-distance work environments and consider whether you have such cultural differences in your team.

Low power-distance	High power-distance
Team members expect to be consulted	Team members expect to be told what to do
Special privileges for team leaders are not expected	Special privileges for team leaders are expected
Constructive feedback to/disagreement with team leader is expected	Upward feedback from team members to their leader should be avoided
Team leaders need to involve the team in reviewing working practices and codes of conduct	Team leaders need to impose effective working practices and codes of conduct in the team
The empowerment of team members is critical for team success	The buy-in of senior local stakeholders is critical for project success
Team leaders look after the professional needs of team members	Team leaders also look after the needs of team members outside work

A combination of both low power-distance and high power-distance cultural preferences can lead to great synergies in nurturing trust in international teams where trust is fragile. Combining empowerment with respect for status and power is critical for getting things done. However, when these differences are not recognised and respected, the result can be the opposite. Both low power-distance 'consultation' and high power-distance 'respect for authority' can be perceived as 'weak and ineffectual' by the other cultural party.

How are these differences handled in your team? Are they ignored and not respected, leading to misunderstandings and mis-evaluations? Or are they recognised and reconciled so that trust is built? If you are working in a fairly mono-cultural team and such differences are irrelevant, score '0'.

Makes trust in response teams more difficult	-5	-4	-3	-2	-1	0	1	2	3	4	5	Makes trust in response teams easier
This difference is not recognised, discussed, or respected, leading to misunderstandings and mis-evaluations												This difference is recognised, discussed, and respected, so that trust is built

The individual and the group

How do cultural differences concerning the role of the individual and the group impact on your team? Team members from more individualist cultures tend to learn to expect that the interests of the individual will be emphasised over those of the group. They come from smaller nuclear families, and classify themselves and others more by their individual characteristics rather than their group membership. North Americans, Australasians, and Northern Europeans tend to be brought up to have a more individualist approach.

Team members from more collectivist cultures (where the interests of the group are emphasised over those of the individual) tend to learn to expect that the interests of the group will be emphasised over those of the individual. They tend to come from extended families, and from birth onwards are integrated into strong, cohesive groups to which they owe their loyalty. South and South-East Asians, Africans and Middle-Easterners, as well as South Americans tend to have a more collectivist approach.

Look at the following behaviours and beliefs connected to individualist and collectivist work environments and consider whether you have such cultural differences in your team.

Individualist	Collectivist
Team members are accountable only to the team	Team members are accountable to their broader in-groups outside the team
It is necessary to take personal responsibility	It is necessary to assume a joint team responsibility
An individual's own priorities and opinions are distinguished from those of the group	An individual's own priorities and opinions are not distinguished from those of the group
Conflict is inevitable, and if it is well-channelled it can lead to positive outcomes	Conflict should be avoided as it disturbs group harmony and therefore motivation
There is not much of a sense of in-group/out-group; individuals form groups based on common interests or tasks	There is a strong sense of in-group/out-group; a high sense of personal obligation to in-group members; and low or no obligation to out-group members
There is a basic right to privacy	Privacy is less important than close contact with in-groups

A combination of both individualist and collectivist cultural preferences can lead to great synergies in nurturing trust in international teams where trust is fragile. Combining individual accountability with sensitivity to group interests in the wider community is critical for getting things done. However, when these differences are not recognised and respected, the result can be the opposite. An individualist 'I' orientation can be perceived as 'arrogant' and 'disruptive', and a collectivist 'we' orientation can be considered as 'uncommitted' and 'over-cautious'.

How are these differences handled in your team? Are they ignored and not respected, leading to misunderstandings and mis-evaluations? Or are they recognised and reconciled so that trust is built? If you are working in a fairly mono-cultural team and such differences are irrelevant, score '0'.

Makes trust in response teams more difficult												Makes trust in response teams easier
This difference is not recognised, discussed, or respected, leading to misunderstandings and mis-evaluations	-5	-4	-3	-2	-1	0	1	2	3	4	5	This difference is recognised, discussed, and respected, so that trust is built

Time and planning

How do cultural differences in attitudes to time and planning impact on your team? Team members from more single-focus cultures tend to learn that there is one linear path to achieve their objectives. They tend to make a time plan and then stick to it. They also tend to focus on one thing at a time, completing each stage before moving on. North Americans, Australasians, and Northern Europeans tend to be brought up to have a more single-focus approach.

Team members from more multi-focus cultures tend to learn that there are various paths to help achieve objectives, so they should keep options open for as long as possible and emphasise various activities in parallel. They tend to become proficient at multi-tasking, and taking opportunities as they arise. South and South-East Asians, Africans, Middle-Easterners, South Americans, as well as Southern Europeans tend to have a more multi-focus approach.

Look at the behaviours and beliefs connected to single-focus and multi-focus work environments and consider whether you have such cultural differences in your team.

Single-focus	Multi-focus
Value commitment to punctuality, and stick to schedule	Value commitment to relationships, and expect flexibility around timings
Have a low tolerance of interruptions in team meetings (e.g. mobile phones)	Have a high tolerance of interruptions in team meetings – normal working style
Plan ahead for the unexpected, but respond more slowly to changing priorities	Respond quickly and flexibly to changing priorities and opportunities
Stick to agendas and other agreed procedures so as to keep clarity and order	Do not stick to agendas or other agreed procedures if they are no longer practical
Plan activities and execute tasks one at a time	Plan activities and execute tasks in parallel

A combination of both single-focus and multi-focus cultural preferences can lead to great synergies in nurturing trust in international teams where trust is fragile. Combining structured planning with flexibility in response is critical for getting things done. However, when these differences are not recognised and respected, the result can be the opposite. A single-focus approach can be perceived as 'inflexible' and 'pedantic', while a multi-focus approach can be considered as 'time-wasting' and 'disorganised'.

How are these differences handled in your team? Are they ignored and not respected, leading to misunderstandings and mis-evaluations? Or are they recognised and reconciled so that trust is built? If you are working in a fairly mono-cultural team and such differences are irrelevant, score '0'.

Makes trust in response teams more difficult	-5	-4	-3	-2	-1	0	1	2	3	4	5	Makes trust in response teams easier
This difference is not recognised, discussed, or respected, leading to misunderstandings and mis-evaluations												This difference is recognised, discussed, and respected, so that trust is built

3 • How to build trust in teams

One of the key conclusions from the Building Trust Project research was that despite a clear sense of the central importance of trust in the effective operation of emergency-response teams, there were very few tools currently being used that explicitly focused on building trust. It was agreed that in order to build a culture of trust in such team contexts, there needed to be a set of tools (involving a broad range of methodologies) that were clearly and explicitly linked to the issue of trust itself.

The tools that have been developed out of the research (see Section 4) are designed to support teams in building trust in order to:

- help build team awareness and alignment around the issue of trust – through consensus on trust-building preferences, story-telling around shared past experiences, and creating shared group experiences of trust (the focus here is on directly embedding trust in the culture of the team);

- help build a common framework for communicating and working together as a team, with a core focus on cultural and individual differences;

- highlight leadership behaviours explicitly dedicated to the issue of trust-building;

- help fellow team members to get to know each other at a personal level, linked to building deeper trust.

Josh Estey/CARE

South Asia Floods, August 2004, Bangladesh – CARE staff and the Disaster Management Project are helping to bring water to those most in need.

Each tool has a different focus but they can be grouped according to the trust-building needs described above. They are not designed as an integrated package of activities to be worked through one by one, but as a toolkit of options that can be used to build trust according to the needs of the team and the trust challenges it is facing. They are each linked to the ten criteria for trust (see pages 9–12) and may be particularly useful at different phases in the life-cycle of an emergency-response team.

Integrating trust-building into humanitarian action

The ability to integrate the trust-building tools into the planning of an emergency response is critical for humanitarian agencies.

This section shows how teams can use the trust-building tools at 'strategic' moments in the emergency-planning cycle in order to improve team effectiveness and programme delivery.

Emergency-response planning, for most agencies, is divided into four phases: preparedness, response, recovery, and transition. During each of these phases, agencies strategise, organise, and respond in the communities where they are working. As some agencies work through local partners, they may not have technical capacities to assist in the event of an emergency, but these agencies may still offer financial support and/or advocate on policy issues that arise from emergencies.

Even though agencies may respond in different ways or are structured differently, the four phases below form the working definition for emergency management.

El Fasher, North Darfur, 2007 – integrated response.

- **Preparedness:** can include organisational capacity-building activities related to disaster risk-reduction (at field and regional level) as well as those pre-deployment activities that take place immediately before an emergency.

- **Response:** this is the phase when humanitarian organisations send assessment teams to the crisis site and begin to assemble resources (human and financial) to respond to an emergency. Based on the baseline assessment, agencies evaluate internal as well as local capacities for an emergency response. During this phase, teams are formed (often comprised of national and international staff) at the field level, to save lives and protect livelihoods.

- **Recovery:** this is often referred to as the rehabilitation phase, when project implementation continues with ongoing response activities, and changes in emergency-response teams occur (e.g. temporary staff begin to disassemble whilst permanent and international staff continue). In addition during this phase, longer-term project-planning occurs, after-action reviews are planned, and agencies in partnership with local communities begin to restore their livelihoods.

- **Transition:** this is the bridge between rehabilitation and creating longer-term sustainable development strategies.[2]

(NB These commonly accepted four emergency phases offer the basis for planning within the humanitarian relief sector. As a result of conflict and chronic natural and/or manmade disasters as well as the complexity of the humanitarian operating environment, one phase does not necessarily 'end' and the next phase automatically begin. These four phases should be understood as the frame for organisational alignment during an emergency response.)

The figure below offers emergency managers a practical way of inserting the trust-building tools into their emergency planning.

The top tier of boxes represents the evolutionary cycle of an emergency response. The four boxes on the bottom are the corresponding team-development stages when trust-building tools can be integrated into the working environment.

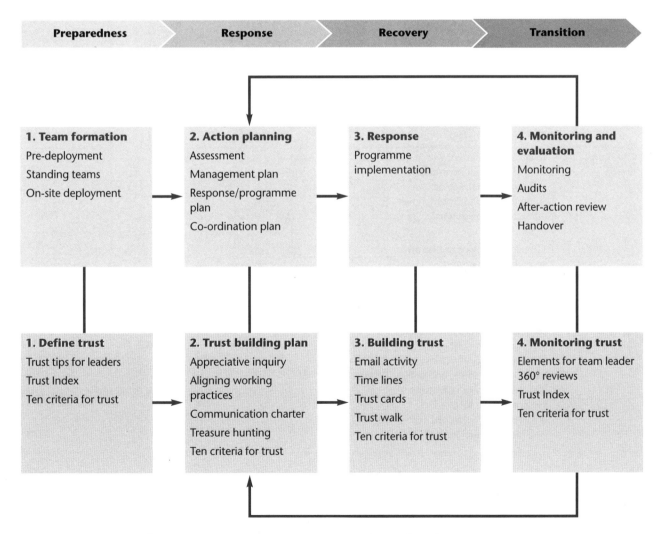

| Preparedness | Response | Recovery | Transition |

1. Team formation
Pre-deployment
Standing teams
On-site deployment

2. Action planning
Assessment
Management plan
Response/programme plan
Co-ordination plan

3. Response
Programme implementation

4. Monitoring and evaluation
Monitoring
Audits
After-action review
Handover

1. Define trust
Trust tips for leaders
Trust Index
Ten criteria for trust

2. Trust building plan
Appreciative inquiry
Aligning working practices
Communication charter
Treasure hunting
Ten criteria for trust

3. Building trust
Email activity
Time lines
Trust cards
Trust walk
Ten criteria for trust

4. Monitoring trust
Elements for team leader
360° reviews
Trust Index
Ten criteria for trust

[2] Often at this stage a new team is formed to take over from the emergency-response team. It is therefore important to begin a new cycle of using the trust-building tools.

Linking the trust tools to the four phases of emergency response

The table below lists the trust tools (in the left-hand column) and describes each tool's purpose. The next columns indicate how useful each particular tool is at different stages of an emergency response.

Tools	Purposes	Phase 1 (Preparedness)	Phase 2 (Response)	Phase 3 (Recovery)	Phase 4 (Transition)
Trust tips for leaders	To remind team leaders of some key behaviours and activities that they can use to promote trust within their teams	very useful	useful	useful	useful
Appreciative inquiry	To create energy and common commitment to building trust in practical ways, which team members know from experience have worked in the past To support the building of alignment as a factor supporting trust in the team	useful	very useful	useful	useful
Aligning working practices	To bring to the surface diverse assumptions of team members about how they expect to work together, and agree on ground rules for moving forward To build trust by understanding the logic behind diverse cultural behaviours, while moving towards commonality	N/A	very useful	useful	N/A
Communication charter	To achieve alignment within the team about what information and opinions need to be communicated to whom, how often, and through what channels To build trust by providing an agreed and structured framework for communication within the team	N/A	very useful	useful	N/A
Treasure hunting	To help team members appreciate the gifts and qualities that each person brings to the team, and to see the diversity of background, culture, and skills that are available in the team. Personal trust is fostered by breaking the ice that can exist in new multi-cultural teams	N/A	very useful	useful	useful

Tools	Purpose(s)	Phase 1 (Preparedness)	Phase 2 (Response)	Phase 3 (Recovery)	Phase 4 (Transition)
Email activity	To build trust through encouraging a discussion of different communication styles that may exist within the team, and how to reconcile them	N/A	very useful	useful	N/A
Time lines	To help team members get to know each other at a deeper level, including values, motivations, and significant life events. Trust is built by allowing people to make themselves vulnerable, and take this risk together	N/A	very useful	useful	useful
Trust cards	To gain the commitment of all team members to an initial trust vision involving a statement of desired behaviours and a visualisation To support the building of alignment as a factor supporting trust in the team	N/A	very useful	useful	useful
Trust walk	To introduce a common experience to enable team members to explore together what factors enhance and destroy trust	N/A	useful	very useful	useful
Elements for team leader 360° reviews	To assist team leaders in assessing their contribution toward the building of trust within emergency-response teams	N/A	N/A	useful	very useful

40

4 • The trust-building tools

Guidance notes

The trust-building tools found in this section form the basis for building trust in diverse teams during an emergency response. These tools consist of practical, field-tested activities that team leaders/facilitators can use with their teams at different stages.

There are ten tools. Each tool is divided into six sections:

1. **Learning objectives:** outlines purpose and expected outcomes for the team
2. **Overview:** provides brief background and outline of the tool
3. **Session plan:** presents session-planning guidelines and resources required, and highlights areas addressed in the ten criteria for trust and Trust Index
4. **How it works:** explains how the tool should be introduced and presented to the team
5. **Facilitation tips:** offers useful suggestions on how to get the best out of the tool
6. **Links to the ten criteria for trust:** highlights links to the criteria so that the facilitator knows which areas the tool addresses

(NB Tools 7 and 8 do not include session plans, facilitation tips, or links to the ten criteria for trust as they are guidelines for managers rather than team-orientated tools).

The trust-building tools are grouped thematically as follows:

Group One – building a common trust platform

*   Appreciative inquiry (Tool 1: page 44)
*   Trust cards: (Tool 2: page 48)
*   Trust walk (Tool 3: page 65)

This set of tools helps to build team awareness and alignment around the issue of trust – through consensus on trust-building preferences, common elements of past experience, and a shared group experience. These tools focus directly on embedding trust in the culture of the team. They are particularly useful for working on the Alignment factors in the Trust Index (see page 28).

Group Two – bridging diversity principles with working practices

*   Communication charter: (Tool 4: page 70)
*   Aligning working practices: (Tool 5: page 79)
*   Email activity: (Tool 6: page 86)

This set of tools helps to build a common framework for communicating and working together as a team, with an explicit focus on cultural and individual differences at the core. They are particularly useful for working on the Organisational, Alignment, and Cultural factors in the Trust Index (see pages 24, 28, and 30).

Group Three – putting trust in leadership

Trust tips for team leaders: (Tool 7: page 95)

Elements for team leader 360° reviews (Tool 8: page 106)

This set of tools identifies leadership behaviours explicitly dedicated to the issue of trust-building. The tools are directly linked to the Leadership factors in the Trust Index (see page 26).

Group Four – promoting inclusiveness

Treasure hunting (Tool 9: page 110)

Time lines: (Tool 10: page 114)

This set of tools encourages fellow team members to get to know each other at a personal level, linked to building deeper trust. They are particularly useful for working on the Team-composition factors in the Trust Index (see page 27).

Within the session-plan section of each tool, an indication is given of the level of facilitation required (high, medium, or low). The table below defines each level.

Facilitation level required

High	Medium	Low
Variety of methods required within one activity, including building consensus and facilitating group discussion in diverse group contexts	Less variety of methods and complexity of facilitation skills needed. But still a requirement to generate group discussion and to link trust issues back to the team's development needs	A simple activity requiring a strict adherence to the trainer notes rather than any more advanced facilitation skills

Tool 1: Appreciative inquiry

Learning objectives

The purpose of this tool is to:

- discover how trust can be built in the emergency-response team;
- build commitment among team members to the process of monitoring and building trust;
- energise and create enthusiasm about what it could be like in the team if levels of mutual trust and respect were high.

Overview

This investigation into how trust could be built in a specific team uses an approach called appreciative inquiry. The process focuses on the positive aspects of 'what works' and is quite distinct from other problem-solving approaches applied in bringing about change in organisations. Some key assumptions that lie behind this process are:

1. In every society, organisation, or group, some things work. Let's focus on what we do that works instead of what doesn't work.
2. What we focus on becomes our reality.
3. People have more confidence and are more comfortable to journey into the future (the unknown) when they carry forward parts of the past (the known).
4. If we carry parts of the past forward, they should be what is best about the past.
5. It is important to value differences.
6. The language we use creates our reality.

The process relies on using the positive experiences of the team members to identify the common themes present in these situations where team members have experienced high levels of trust in the past. It relies on story-telling around two central questions:

Describe a time when you were part of a team that had a high level of trust and respect among the members and from those outside the team. How were trust and respect built and communicated? What made it possible to establish trust in this group?

This tool can be used at any time to help team members build trust, but can be particularly useful for a team that has started work and has some experience of working together. The process itself will create energy and common commitment to building trust in practical ways which team members know from experience have worked in the past.

Session plan

Overall time required	2.5 hours (NB This activity can be split into two parts)
Group size	8 +
Level of facilitation required	High
Relevant trust index items	Alignment (A number of other aspects of the Trust Index may be relevant depending on the content of the individual stories told)
Resources required	Copies of the ten criteria for trust for facilitator reference Flip-chart paper and marker pens (to pre-write instructions and record stories) Notepads, pens, and pencils (for interviewers) Tape or blu-tack to post the flip-charts around the room

How it works

1. Introduce the objectives of the session and the ideas behind appreciative inquiry:
    *   focusing on the positive and things that work
    *   using the experiences of team members
    *   story-telling
    *   identifying common themes
    *   creating 'provocative propositions'.

2. Show the following statement and questions on the pre-written flip-chart:

    Describe a time when you were part of a team that had a high level of trust and respect among the members and from those outside the team. How were trust and respect built and communicated? What made it possible to establish trust in this group?

3. Ask everyone to work on their own for 10–15 minutes to recall the details of a time when they experienced a team with good levels of trust.

4. Split the participants into pairs, making sure that, as far as possible, differences within the team are bridged within the pairs (e.g. national and international, younger and older, male and female).

5. Ask each pair to interview each other to get the details of their trust story. Encourage them to get involved with each others' story to create mutual energy and enthusiasm. Make sure that the interviewers are curious and ask open questions to get as much detail as possible. Usually they should be able to generate their own questions, but if they need some help you could suggest the following:
    A. What was it about the situation that allowed trust to be high?
    B. What was it about you at that time that enabled you to share in this experience?
    C. What did people do to create trust?
    D. What was the role of the leader or leaders in building trust?
    E. What was it about the team's task that helped them to build trust?
    F. What did you notice about the effectiveness of the team in performing its task? Why was this?
    G. What were your feelings when you worked in that team?
    H. What was the team's relationship with its environment (e.g. other teams, the organisation etc.) and how did this contribute to trust within the team?

6. Make sure that the interviewer keeps notes of the elements of the story that are interesting/exciting/useful/memorable. Suggest they copy down some actual quotes if possible.

7. When the 'interviews' are complete, gather the whole team into groups of about seven or eight people. Where possible, put members of each original pair in different groups.

8. After the groups have formed, ask each person in each group to recount the story they have been told by their partner. Each group should appoint a recorder whose job it is to make notes of the key features of each story, preferably on a flip-chart that everyone can see. In this way the group can compile a set of words, quotes, and ideas about the common elements of the stories.

A possible break in the activity can be taken here.

9. *[An alternative to the process described in step 8 above is to ask each person, working on their own, to prepare a summary of the story they have heard on no more than two sides of A4 paper. Once this has been done, collect all the written stories. If necessary, the session can be ended here and resumed at a later date. If there is a break between sessions, prepare copies of the stories and circulate copies to all members of the team so that everyone has a copy of everyone else's story. When the session resumes, split the whole team into groups of seven or eight people and give them the task of identifying the common themes and elements from all the stories that have been circulated.]*

10. Place the results of each group's discussions on flip-chart paper around the room for all to see. Give people a chance to wander around and read all the different ideas.

11. Ask each group to use the key themes that have been identified to prepare 'proposition' statements. Proposition statements are statements about how the team proposes to work together. They can convey the underlying sentiments that emerged from the flip-chart exercise, or they can be based on how the team currently perceives they work together. They should:

    • use the evidence from all the stories that have been told by the members of the whole team;

    • encapsulate the key truths from those stories in short, provocative statements (one theme per set of statements). Short statements of one sentence are often the most valuable, because they can be easily remembered and repeated;

    • express each truth as if it is true for their team already (affirmative and in the present tense) e.g. 'We build trust by expressing our concerns directly to the people that they are aimed at'.

12. As facilitator you may have to help the teams craft the propositions. The objective is to help them take what they know and talk about what could be. Use the following criteria to judge whether each proposition is valid:

    • Is it provocative? Does it stretch us? Does it challenge us? Is it innovative?

    • Is it grounded in the stories that have been told and the examples that have been given?

    • Is it what we want? Will people defend it or get passionate about it?

    • Is it stated in affirmative, bold terms and in the present tense – as if it were already happening?

13. When all the propositions are complete, hang the flip-chart paper around the room and ask different people to read out all the statements – with passion.

14. The process of working together to prepare these statements is as important as the final output. Encourage the team to take these propositions and publicise them in some way so that the team can refer to them and be reminded of what they decided.

Facilitation tips

- The facilitator's objective throughout this process is to build energy and passion around the theme of trust and how to create it. This should begin to build when team members begin to see the common themes from all the stories.

- You may need to help the groups in framing their propositions, especially if there is limited fluency in the working language for some participants within the group. Creating text that is challenging and engaging for the team requires some skill in writing. Be sure not to impose your own ideas.

- If there is time, you can use the trust propositions as a platform for discussing where the team's strengths/gaps might be in relation to trust.

- Make sure that the trust propositions produced by the team are behavioural. Try to avoid abstract statements such as: 'We build trust in our team by respecting each other…'. Get to the behaviour by asking questions such as: 'How would we show this 'respect'…'?

- Connect the propositions with the ten criteria for trust where relevant. This builds confidence that the truths about trust come from within the experience of the team rather than from outside.

- If you are working with smaller groups of around six people you can have just one group at stages 7–8.

- If you are working with larger teams (of more than 14 people) you can start the process with the leadership group, and then cascade it down. As a final stage you can share the trust propositions from each group, and synthesise them down to one set.

Links to the ten criteria for trust

Any or all of the ten criteria for trust may become relevant in this exercise, depending on the content of the individual stories told.

Tool 2: Trust cards

Learning objectives

The purpose of this tool is to:

*   identify a range of behaviours that can be used to build trust within the emergency-response team;

*   identify the key elements of trust that the team members feel are most important for them;

*   gain the commitment of all team members to adopting five high-priority behaviours when working in the team.

Overview

The activity uses some pre-formatted trust cards and some blank cards. It enables the team members to generate ideas about what would build trust within their emergency-response team, and then to prioritise these ideas. The participants work first in pairs, then in groups of four, and finally as a whole group to select the number of cards the team as a whole judges to be most important. Having agreed on the most important five items, the team then works to consider how they apply in practice to the work of the team. Individuals also consider what they need to do differently to better comply with these key trust behaviours, and then they publicly commit to adopting those behaviours.

The activity requires the use of 50 cards which need to be printed in advance and which are provided in Handout 2a on page 51. In addition, one blank card will need to be provided for each participant. The blank cards are also pre-formatted (in Handout 2b on page 64).

The activity will normally be run in two sessions, with some time between each meeting. (It can be carried out in one long session if time permits.) Timings will depend to some extent on the size of the group, which can be any number up to 25. Typically the first session usually lasts for about one hour and the second session lasts for about one and a half hours.

Session plan

Overall time required	2.5 hours in total. (NB This activity is split into two parts with individuals working on their own between the two sessions)
Group size	10–25
Level of facilitation required	Medium
Relevant Trust Index items	Team composition Alignment Leadership
Resources required	Copies of the ten criteria for trust for facilitator reference A set of 50 trust cards (Handout 2a) A set of blank trust cards (Handout 2b) Flip-chart paper, coloured marker pens, pens and pencils, old newspapers and magazines (to create a visual image and written trust statement)

How it works – first session

1. Introduce the activity and the learning objectives.
2. Go over the ten criteria for trust with descriptions and give examples of each.
3. Give one blank trust card to each participant and ask them to complete it with 'one thing that is essential for me personally to trust others in this team'.
4. Team members should be asked not to talk among themselves at this stage.
5. Collect all of the cards, place them face down on the floor or table and invite each person to take one. It does not make any difference if a person picks their own card, the exercise proceeds.
6. Shuffle the 50 trust cards and give two to each person, so that everyone has three cards in total.
7. Form the group into pairs. It is preferrable if each person is paired with someone who they will be seeing and/or working with before the next session.

How it works – between sessions

1. Before the next meeting each person is asked to rank the three cards they hold in order of their importance to that person.
2. Each person then gets together with their partner and they share their ranking of the trust cards. Together they must reduce their six trust cards to just the two which reflect what is most important for both of them.

How it works – second session

1. Arrange for each pair to meet with another pair. This new group of four must now reduce their four cards to two. If it is a particularly large group then three pairs can come together and reduce their six cards to two.
2. Now re-assemble the whole group and ask them to negotiate together to reduce the final number of cards on which they can all agree to five in total. If necessary help them with a process to achieve this (see Facilitation tips overleaf).
3. When the list of five items has been agreed, split the group into two equal halves. Ask one group to create a picture for each of the five cards which visualises how the items are connected and relevant to the work of the team. Invite the other group to prepare a short written statement of what behaviours the team expects from every member in order for there to be a very high level of trust.
4. Ask each group to present the results of their work to the other, and press each to explain how the five factors will look in practice in the context of their team.
5. Ask everyone to work on their own for five minutes to identify two or three things about their own behaviour that they will seek to change in order to comply with these trust priorities. Ask each person in turn to explain and commit to making some personal changes.

Building Trust in Diverse Teams

Facilitation tips

- Make sure that you prepare the cards in advance. If the group is small you may want to reduce the number of cards that you will shuffle to ensure that each of the ten criteria for trust are reasonably represented in the cards distributed. The number in brackets after each behaviour on each card represents the criteria to which it relates (numbers 1–10). If for example you need to reduce the number of cards to 20, then choose two questions from criterion 1, two from criterion 2 and so on.

- It is best to have people working in pairs at the initial stages; depending on the number of participants, groups of three may be more convenient.

- You may want to pair national and international team members together either in the first or second stage to make sure that any cultural differences are brought to the surface as part of the prioritisation process.

- For the session where the final five items are selected, allow the team to work out their own process to arrive at this conclusion, if possible. Suggest that it must be a consensus decision and that the voices of the quieter members of the group need to be taken into account on an equal basis with those of the more outspoken members. If they find this difficult you could suggest a process. (E.g. list the items on a flip-chart and allow each person five votes which they can use to indicate the items they support. When everyone has voted, the items with the least number of votes are eliminated, and the process repeated until there are only five items left.)

- Don't worry too much about getting the 'correct' top five items. The process of thinking and discussing is more important than the particular five chosen.

- Have some old newspapers and magazines available in case the group who will prepare the visualisation requires them.

- When the group splits into two halves in the final session, let people choose which group they wish to join, but insist that the numbers in each group be roughly equal.

Links to the ten criteria for trust

The trust behaviours chosen by the team will be aligned with the ten criteria for trust.

This tool is reproduced with permission from WorldWork Limited

Handout 2a: Trust Cards

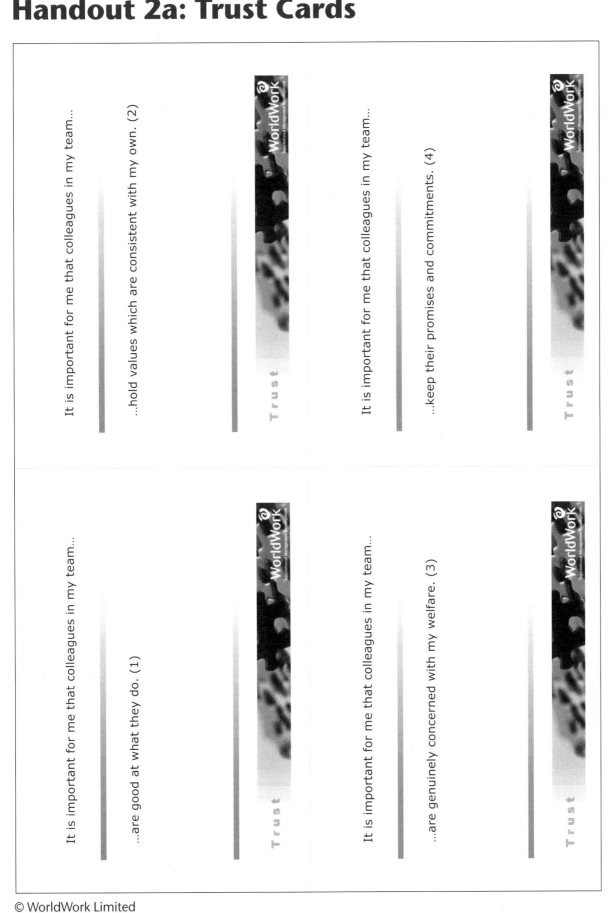

It is important for me that colleagues in my team...

...hold values which are consistent with my own. (2)

Trust

It is important for me that colleagues in my team...

...keep their promises and commitments. (4)

Trust

It is important for me that colleagues in my team...

...are good at what they do. (1)

Trust

It is important for me that colleagues in my team...

...are genuinely concerned with my welfare. (3)

Trust

© WorldWork Limited

Handout 2a: Trust Cards

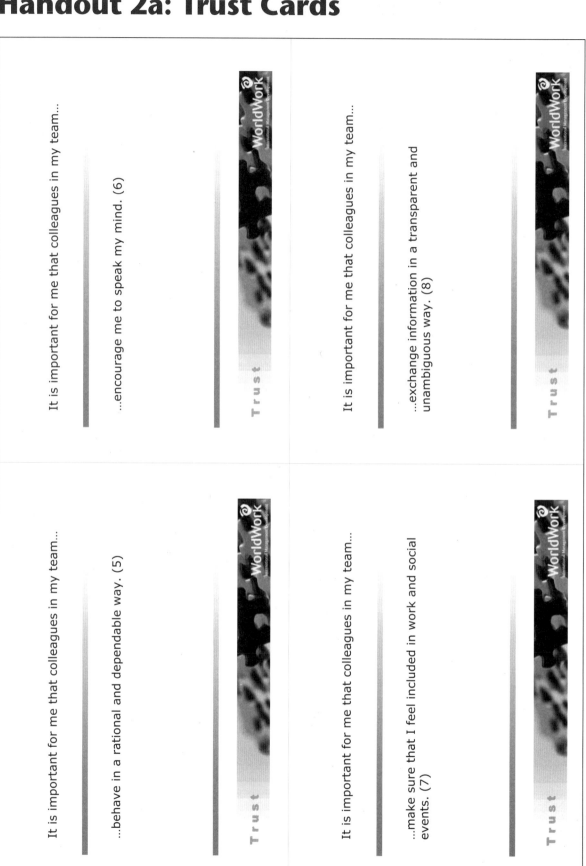

It is important for me that colleagues in my team...

...encourage me to speak my mind. (6)

Trust

It is important for me that colleagues in my team...

...exchange information in a transparent and unambiguous way. (8)

Trust

It is important for me that colleagues in my team...

...behave in a rational and dependable way. (5)

Trust

It is important for me that colleagues in my team...

...make sure that I feel included in work and social events. (7)

Trust

Handout 2a: Trust Cards

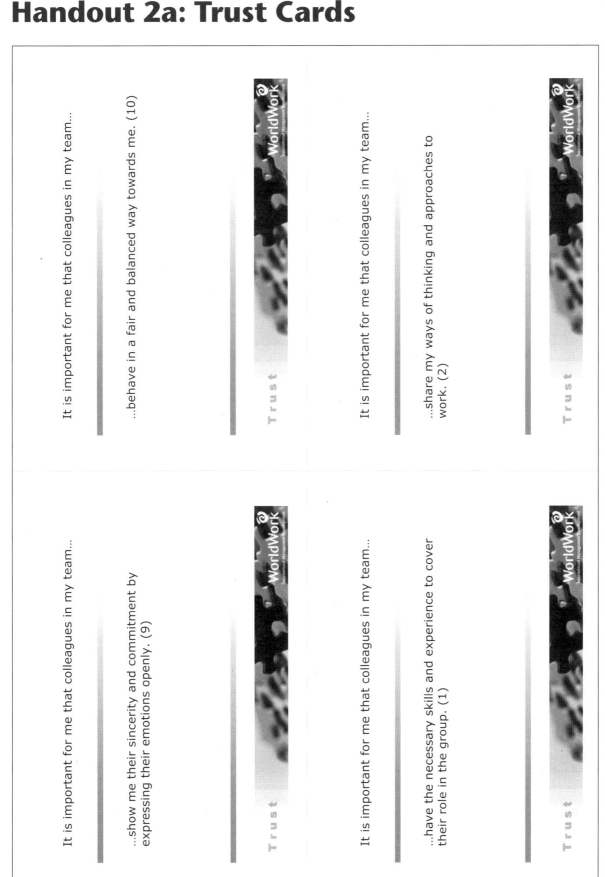

It is important for me that colleagues in my team...

...behave in a fair and balanced way towards me. (10)

Trust

It is important for me that colleagues in my team...

...share my ways of thinking and approaches to work. (2)

Trust

It is important for me that colleagues in my team...

...show me their sincerity and commitment by expressing their emotions openly. (9)

Trust

It is important for me that colleagues in my team...

...have the necessary skills and experience to cover their role in the group. (1)

Trust

Handout 2a: Trust Cards

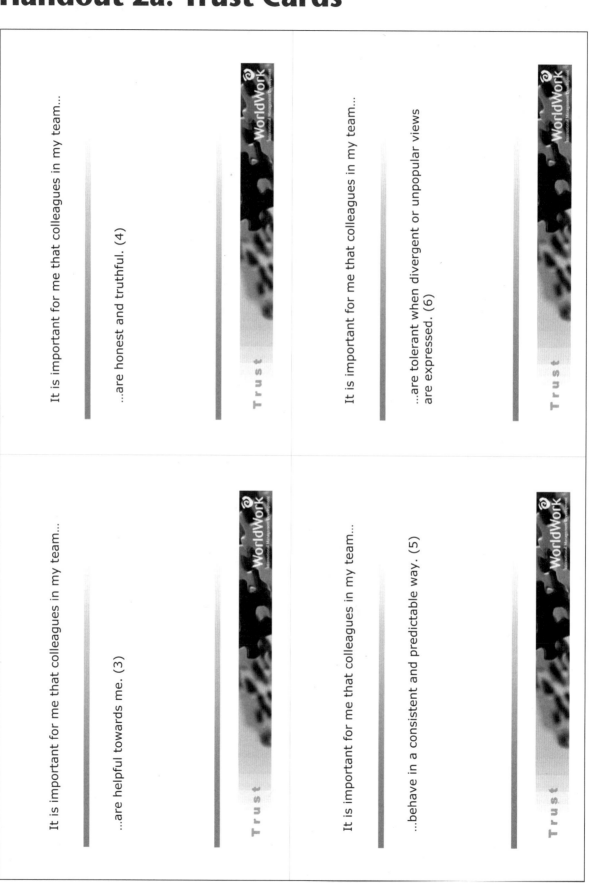

It is important for me that colleagues in my team...

...are honest and truthful. (4)

Trust

It is important for me that colleagues in my team...

...are tolerant when divergent or unpopular views are expressed. (6)

Trust

It is important for me that colleagues in my team... (3)

...are helpful towards me. (3)

Trust

It is important for me that colleagues in my team...

...behave in a consistent and predictable way. (5)

Trust

Handout 2a: Trust Cards

It is important for me that colleagues in my team...

...are open about their needs and motives. (8)

Trust

It is important for me that colleagues in my team...

...are mutually supportive of efforts to achieve our common goals. (10)

Trust

It is important for me that colleagues in my team...

...take decisions in a participative and democratic way. (7)

Trust

It is important for me that colleagues in my team...

...are emotionally an 'open book' – their feelings are easy to read. (9)

Trust

Building Trust in Diverse Teams

Handout 2a: Trust Cards

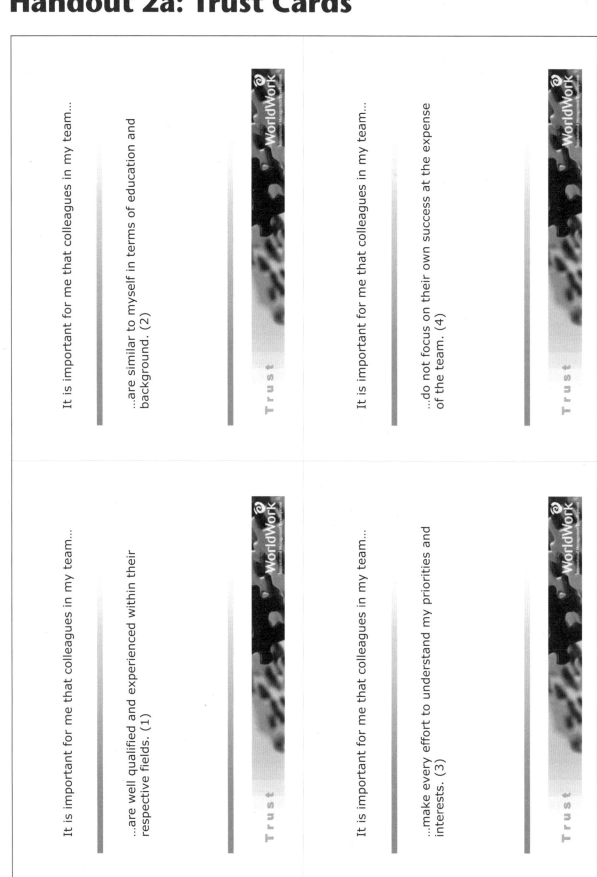

It is important for me that colleagues in my team...

...are well qualified and experienced within their respective fields. (1)

It is important for me that colleagues in my team...

...are similar to myself in terms of education and background. (2)

It is important for me that colleagues in my team...

...make every effort to understand my priorities and interests. (3)

It is important for me that colleagues in my team...

...do not focus on their own success at the expense of the team. (4)

Trust

WorldWork

Handout 2a: Trust Cards

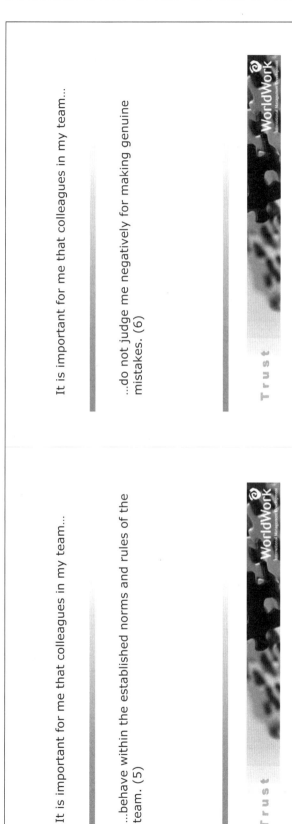

It is important for me that colleagues in my team...

...do not judge me negatively for making genuine mistakes. (6)

Trust

It is important for me that colleagues in my team...

...do not hide useful information from other members of the team. (8)

Trust

It is important for me that colleagues in my team...

...behave within the established norms and rules of the team. (5)

Trust

It is important for me that colleagues in my team...

...are ready to share their successes with me. (7)

Trust

Group One • Tool 2: Trust cards • Handout 2a

Handout 2a: Trust Cards

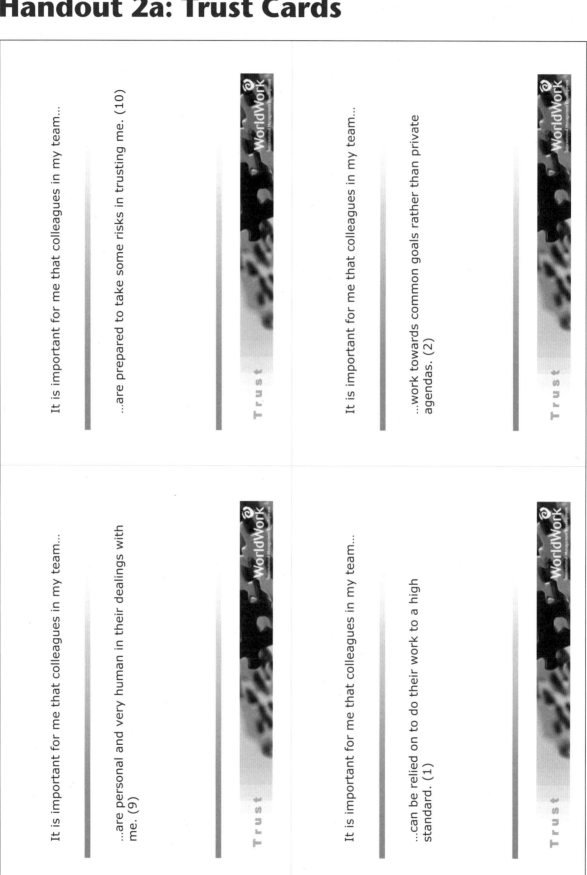

It is important for me that colleagues in my team...

...are prepared to take some risks in trusting me. (10)

Trust

It is important for me that colleagues in my team...

...work towards common goals rather than private agendas. (2)

Trust

It is important for me that colleagues in my team...

...are personal and very human in their dealings with me. (9)

Trust

It is important for me that colleagues in my team...

...can be relied on to do their work to a high standard. (1)

Trust

Handout 2a: Trust Cards

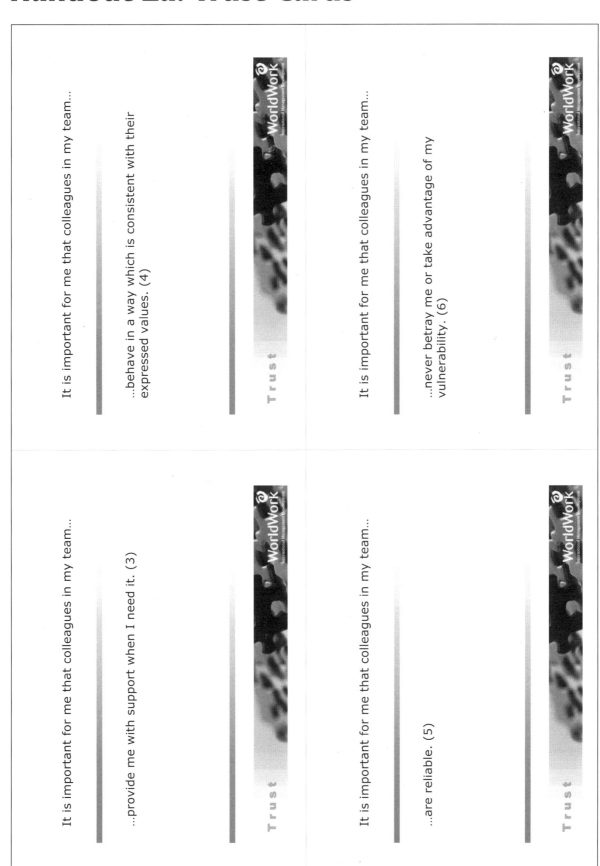

It is important for me that colleagues in my team...

...behave in a way which is consistent with their expressed values. (4)

Trust

It is important for me that colleagues in my team...

...never betray me or take advantage of my vulnerability. (6)

Trust

It is important for me that colleagues in my team...

...provide me with support when I need it. (3)

Trust

It is important for me that colleagues in my team...

...are reliable. (5)

Trust

Handout 2a: Trust Cards

It is important for me that colleagues in my team...

...make themselves available and are approachable and responsive. (8)

Trust

WorldWork

It is important for me that colleagues in my team...

...frequently co-operate with me when working to achieve our respective goals. (10)

Trust

WorldWork

It is important for me that colleagues in my team...

...listen and positively respond to my ideas and opinions. (7)

Trust

WorldWork

It is important for me that colleagues in my team...

...are ready to reveal personal information about themselves. (9)

Trust

WorldWork

Handout 2a: Trust Cards

It is important for me that colleagues in my team...

...use a shared 'language' or code of communication with which I am familiar. (2)

Trust

It is important for me that colleagues in my team...

...consistently support the team even when under pressure not to. (4)

Trust

It is important for me that colleagues in my team...

...have a reputation for performing successfully in their respective fields. (1)

Trust

It is important for me that colleagues in my team...

...do not take advantage of me even when I am vulnerable. (3)

Trust

Building Trust in Diverse Teams

Handout 2a: Trust Cards

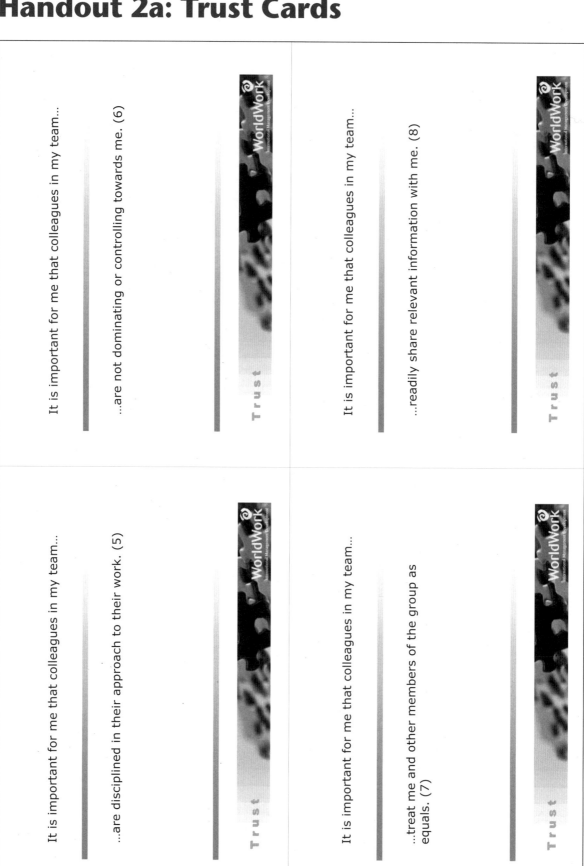

It is important for me that colleagues in my team...

...are disciplined in their approach to their work. (5)

Trust

It is important for me that colleagues in my team...

...are not dominating or controlling towards me. (6)

Trust

It is important for me that colleagues in my team...

...treat me and other members of the group as equals. (7)

Trust

It is important for me that colleagues in my team...

...readily share relevant information with me. (8)

Trust

Handout 2a: Trust Cards

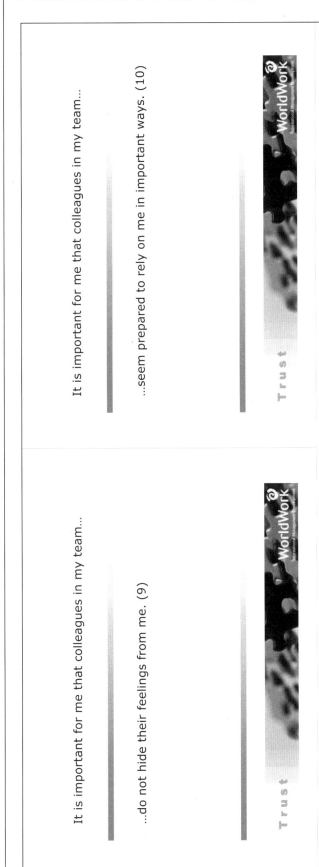

It is important for me that colleagues in my team...

...seem prepared to rely on me in important ways. (10)

Trust

It is important for me that colleagues in my team...

...do not hide their feelings from me. (9)

Trust

Handout 2b: Blank Trust Cards

© WorldWork Limited

Tool 3: Trust walk

Learning objectives

The purpose of this tool is to:

- provide a safe and fun activity in which team members have to start relying on and trusting each other;

- create a context in which team members can experiment with trust and reflect on the experience and the nature of trust;

- introduce a common experience to enable team members to explore together what factors enhance and destroy trust.

Overview

The activity consists of the team walking together along a pre-determined route while blindfolded. Team members form a line, one in front of the other, and each person either places one hand on the shoulder of the person in front or holds onto a rope which connects team members together. Whilst walking the trust walk route, the team is guided by one or more guides using a limited set of communication signals.

After the walk is completed, team members are encouraged to think about the experience and what they have learned from it that will help them work together in the emergency-response team. It is an excellent way to analyse and build the emotional component of trust, and thus is a good team-building tool.

Session plan

Overall time required	1–2 hours
Group size	8–15
Level of facilitation required	Medium
Relevant Trust Index items	Team composition Alignment
Resources required	Copies of the ten critieria for trust for facilitator reference Copies of Handout 3a: Links to the ten criteria for trust Clean blindfolds for each person One or two long ropes Stakes and ribbons to mark the course Flip-chart paper, stand, and markers Access to a space (preferably outside) where the walk can take place

How it works

1. Before the session, set out a challenging and varied route that will take the blindfolded participants about 20 minutes to complete. It can be inside or outside, although outside is preferable. If the exercise is conducted outside, arrange for the group to navigate around trees and over a log or two; go through some bushes; crawl over and under an obstacle; walk next to water (which you can splash so it is heard or felt without causing a hazard!). To increase the challenge, include crossing a bridge or going down a drop. If the exercise is conducted inside, place chairs, desks, and other objects around the room. Put balls of paper or other 'crunchy' material underfoot so that it creates a difference in texture and/or sound effect. Whether inside or outside, make sure that the route allows all team members to participate (see Facilitation tips on page 68 for more on this).

2. Introduce the exercise to the whole team and set it in context. Explain the learning objectives (e.g. research has identified that a culture of trust amongst staff is one of the most important factors in an agency's ability to launch and implement a timely and effective emergency response).

3. This particular exercise is designed to:
    *   build trust between team members;
    *   explore what trust means;
    *   help team members get to know each other better.

4. Explain that the participants will not only experience the exercise but they will also need to recall how they felt during the experience, so that they can discuss it afterwards.

5. Emphasise the importance of taking the exercise slowly. If anyone should feel unsafe, the activity can be stopped temporarily to address the issue. Have a signal for this (e.g. both hands raised, or a key word).

6. This element of the exercise is optional and can be left out if time is short. Divide into groups of three or four and ask each group:
    *   to list what trust means to them; and
    *   from this, to identify what is required to develop trust.

    Reconvene the whole group and share results briefly. Use this opportunity to introduce the links to the ten criteria for trust. Distribute Handout 3a. Explain that you will revisit their lists and discuss the links to the criteria after the exercise.

    (NB This step could be done while the facilitator is briefing the guides in step 11.)

7. Explain that the objective is to get the whole team to navigate through an obstacle course. The challenge is that they will all be blindfolded except for two guides. You might wish to invent a story to make it more interesting or real. For example: 'You are a tour party about to cross a sacred area and you are not allowed to look at it. Therefore you must be blindfolded and guided by two elders…'.

    (NB In cultures with taboos about members of the opposite sex touching, or if you wish to raise gender issues, you can divide the group into men and women for the exercise. In this case the 'sacred area' is sacred for men/women.)

8. Check that the group is OK about being blindfolded. Emphasise that you will be present to ensure their safety. Remind them about the 'safety' gesture or word.

9. The facilitator or the group should choose two team members to serve as guides. Explain that you are going to take the guides to see the route and that while away the group(s) should spend some time planning how they will approach the activity. If applicable, point out they can use the rope.

10. Explain to everyone that the guides will not be allowed to say anything or communicate with the blindfolded group in normal language. They can make whatever sounds they like, e.g. whistles, clucking, clapping etc. in order to guide the team. Also, they are not allowed to touch any members of the group so, obviously, a means of communication must be established in a minimum amount of time.

11. Take the guides and show them the route. Only they can see the markers. Give them a few minutes away from the group to establish and agree their communication signals. Return to the group with the guides and remind everyone of the rules:

    • No speaking, only sounds as a means of communication

    • The guides cannot touch them

12. Ask everyone to put on their blindfolds. Go round and check that everyone is OK and that they cannot see anything. When ready, give a signal to start the walk.

13. The duration of the walk will depend on the degree of difficulty of the obstacle course and the skill of the group.

14. Join the trust walkers on the walk. Watch for potential danger and make sure you are in a good position at all times. Point out the route to the guides if they lose their way. Watch and listen for situations that will be valuable to relate during the post-trip discussion. Make notes if necessary.

15. Try to end up in an area that allows the group to be physically close together. Announce that they have arrived at the destination and the blindfolds can be removed.

16. When the team has completed the course, ask the guides to walk the group back through the route to satisfy their curiosity and allow spontaneous sharing of reactions and sensations.

17. Debrief the session. Review the ten criteria for trust with the group. During this discussion, revisit the original trust list from step 6 and revise it if necessary. Document the main points on flip-charts. Some of the following questions can be useful:

    A. How did it feel to be led?

    B. How did it feel to be a guide?

    C. How and why were the two guides chosen? (If by the group)

    D. Did you rely only on the guides or did you also help each other out?

    E. What did the guides do that helped to get you through the course?

    F. What did you do to help each other through the course?

    G. What kind of communication did you need, to make this work well?

    H. Did you feel that you could trust your guides and the people around you? Why or why not?

    I. What is the relationship between risk and trust?

    J. Did you recognise any gender dynamics?

    K. What lessons can we apply to our work together as an emergency-response team?

    L. What more have we learned about trust? (Refer to their discussion before the exercise if this was included.)

    The facilitator should prepare a summary of the 'lessons learned', using the ideas and thoughts arising from the exercise. This can be typed up and circulated to all participants later.

Facilitation tips

- Safety is of paramount importance. It is your role to ensure that nobody comes to any harm, so you will need to stay close to the group throughout the walk. If there are two groups going at the same time you will need to nominate someone to look after the other group.

- Choose a route that is long enough to enable time for the team to learn and improve as they go. Make it sufficiently difficult to be challenging but not dangerous (e.g. obstacles to navigate round or climb over, hills to climb up, gates to go through etc.). Take into account different physical abilities of the team members and make specific adjustments in the route to ensure that the course is accessible to members of the team with a disability. It should take about 20 minutes to complete the course.

- Emphasise in the briefing that anybody can withdraw from the activity at any time if they are not comfortable. Devise a special word or signal that anyone can use to temporarily halt the process if they need to. Reassure them that you will be watching out for their safety at all times and will stop them if they seem likely to get into trouble.

- Make sure that you do not say anything, and do not allow the guides to say anything that will make anybody appear foolish. Recognise that the team members are all making themselves somewhat vulnerable and as such you must not betray that trust.

- Make sure that there is enough time at the end of this exercise to do a proper debrief of the experience and generate lessons learned linked to trust. Use the ten criteria for trust to help make those links.

- There are a number of options in the way this activity can be run. In particular:
  - The pre-discussion about trust can be omitted.
  - The whole group may work as one team doing the Trust Walk altogether. Alternatively the group can be split into two with one group going round the course one way and the other group going round in the opposite direction.
  - If operating with two groups, the groups can be mixed or split on the basis of gender to allow for taboos about touching members of the opposite sex.
  - Where possible, team members can be connected together by all holding onto a rope with one hand or they can be joined by having each person put one hand on the shoulder of the person in front, or holding hands. Make necessary adjustments if there is a team member with a disability.
  - The guides can be chosen by the group themselves or you can choose them.
  - Participants can be paired at the start of the walk – one is blindfolded and the other is the partner. Partners may hold hands or not as they walk through the course. The pairs go through a similar course – the blindfolded person assisted by their partner through the course on the way out and changing roles and the way back. The same set of questions can be asked at the conclusion.

- Run the debrief at the point where the course ends and run it immediately after the team(s) complete the course whilst the experience is fresh in their minds.

Handout 3a: Links to the ten criteria for trust

Criteria	Definition	Impact of trust walk
Competence	Trust based on a perception that team members are competent, so will not let me down	During the Trust Walk, team members rely on each others' sense of judgement. Often, we question the abilities of our colleagues based on assumptions and do not trust their decisions.
Openness with information	Trust based on the observation that other team members share information important to the team proactively and clearly	Accurate and timely information is essential during an emergency response. The Trust Walk is about trusting that our guide will communicate what we need to know and when we need to know it, so as to secure our journey along the route.
Goodwill	Trust based on the belief that other team members are concerned about my overall welfare	People do not want to be led astray. They want to trust that those around them have their best interests in mind.
Well-being	Trust arising from the feeling that I have nothing to fear from other members of the team	The Trust Walk enables the team to let their guard down and trust that the path they are taking is safe and will lead them in the right direction.

Group One • Tool 3: Trust walk • Handout 3a

Tool 4: Communication charter

Learning objectives

The purpose of this tool is to:

- ensure that all team members understand the role that effective communication can play in building trust within an emergency-response team;

- achieve alignment within the team about what information and opinions need to be communicated to whom, how often, and through which channels;

- provide a structured way for members of the emergency-response team to reach such alignment and to focus on the *process* of communication as well as on the content.

Overview

This tool provides a systematic way for teams to work together to arrive at a plan and agree how communications within the team will work. The team, under the guidance of a facilitator, designs the best strategy for communication amongst team members and then reaches agreement about acceptable behaviours in this respect. Any such plan needs to be reviewed from time to time in the light of changing circumstances.

The creation of a communication charter should be undertaken as early as possible in the life of an emergency-response team. In the early days of a rapid-onset emergency, things will be changing and developing very fast. This will make it difficult to find the time for this activity. However, communication becomes even more crucial in times of change and uncertainty. It is recommended that this tool be used as soon as possible after a team is formed. Regular reviews should be conducted from time to time as the work being undertaken by the emergency-response team changes or as new people become involved in the work.

The creation of a communication charter is best achieved in a team meeting with all team members present. If the team is large, and it is not practical to involve the whole team, then as many of the senior team members as possible should be included. The process could then be repeated in functional or geographical teams later. In practice the total activity could be split into two sessions with team members doing some 'homework' in between the sessions.

The charter itself should take the form of a written document. A simple example is given in Handout 4b. The statements in the charter should be expressed in simple terms in the common working language used by all team members. If language is an issue, the charter could be translated into the local language when complete.

Session plan

Overall time required	3 hours (NB Total time can be reduced to 2 hours 15 minutes by excluding items 4–6 as noted below)
Group size	Whole management team
Level of facilitation required	Medium
Relevant Trust Index items	Organisational Alignment
Resources required	Informal working environment Copies of Handout 4a: Links to the ten criteria for trust Copies of Handout 4b: Communication Charter Example Copies of Handout 4c: Communication Media (optional) Post-it notes in two colours Flip-chart paper, marker pens, and tape/blu-tack

How it works

1. Introduce the session, underlining the importance of good communication to the success of emergency-response teams. Distribute Handout 4a outlining the links between the ten criteria for trust and good communication. Explain that, in this session, the emphasis is on communication *among team members* and with the team leader, not with any outside bodies.

2. Outline the learning objectives and intended output of the session, and start some discussion in the group about the objectives and the charter. Encourage team members to share any initial thoughts about principles that could be adopted. These principles might serve as a guide to decisions about how communications should be structured.

3. Show the group a sample communication charter (Handout 4b) so that they can see what they are aiming at.

4. In a session altogether, discuss and identify the different means of communication that are or will be available to the team. For example these might include:
   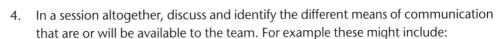
   - team meetings
   - one-to-one meetings
   - regular weekly telephone debriefs
   - ad hoc telephone contact
   - written reports
   - emails
   - voicemail
   - fax
   - bulletin boards – physical or online
   - intranet
   - SMS (text) messages

5. Split the group up into pairs or groups of three and give each group one or more of the above methods to work on. Ask them to identify the advantages and disadvantages of each method and the types of communication for which each is best suited. Ask them to note their answers on flip-charts.

6. Get each sub-group to report back in a session altogether, and encourage questions, discussion, and further suggestions for each method.

A break in the activity can be taken here.

(NB Items 4–6 above could be replaced by a version of the advantages and disadvantages that have been prepared in advance by the facilitator/leader. An example is attached as Handout 4c – but be aware that this will need to be reviewed and adapted in the light of local circumstances. Leaving these steps out will mean that team members are less likely to analyse for themselves the advantages and disadvantages of each communication method).

7. The next step in the process is to identify all the different types of communication that make up the regular exchange of information, views, news, and requests within the team. To achieve this, the facilitator gives each team member two stacks of differently coloured post-it notes. Each team member is then asked:

    *   to write on one colour of post-its all the key information, views, feedback etc. that they need to receive from other team members in order to do their job effectively – one idea on each post-it.

    *   to write on the other colour post-its all the key information, opinion, and feedback that they feel they could usefully provide for other team members – again one idea on each post-it.

    Allow plenty of time for everyone to complete this process. It's a useful way for quieter and more reserved team members to be able to contribute on an equal basis with their more vociferous colleagues.

    (NB Team members could be asked to go away and do this on their own, and come back to another session at a later date when the process will be completed.)

8. Once completed, arrange for all the post-its to be stuck up on a wall. Get all the team to gather together round the wall and work together to cluster the post-its which express the same idea together, and then group all of them under meaningful headings. The team leader should play an important role in this discussion, prompting people for things not included, and suggesting appropriate groupings. The leader needs to be happy with the final result.

9. Split the team into pairs or groups of three and assign each group one or more of the headings identified in 8 above. Their task is to take all the items identified and list them on a flip-chart in a format similar to that shown in Handout 4b. In other words, for each one they need to discuss and agree:

    *   Who should initiate communications of this type?

    *   Who should receive them and who does not need them?

    *   What is the typical content of this type of communication?

    *   What would be the best method of communicating this? (NB Refer back to the output from the initial discussion about the advantages and disadvantages of different methods of communication.)

    *   What priority should communications of this type have?

    *   When should this information be communicated?

Another break in the activity can be taken here.

10. Display the resulting flip-charts around the room and get everyone to walk around and read the results of the other sub-groups. (NB If the option to take a break after step 9 is taken, begin the next session with a brief review of everything that has been done up to then.) In a session altogether, provide an opportunity for questions and challenges to the results. Ask the group to look for any inconsistencies between the outputs of the different groups. Resolve these through discussion.

11. Ask each team member to write down in one or two bullet points the commitments that they make to the team. They should:
    - identify the people in the team that they particularly need to improve their communications with;
    - consider which elements of the communication charter grid they need to focus on;
    - state specifically what they undertake to do or to do differently as a result of being involved in the process of preparing the charter.

12. Ask for a volunteer to type up the results into a unified charter and distribute it to all those present.

Facilitation tips

- This should be a participative process in which all team members play a part. It works best and is most useful where there is a degree of inter-dependence in the work of the different group members, as would normally be the case in a management team.

- Choose a setting which is not formal and is preferably away from where normal business meetings take place. It is important to create the impression that this is something important and different from normal day-to-day work. Existing habits, and assumptions about hierarchical relationships, power differences, cliques within the team etc. are weakened during the process. The process is strengthened when it takes place on a 'level playing field'.

- It is important to keep the items to be included in the charter at a workable level. If too many individual items are included, the exercise will become too long and complicated. The overall purpose may be lost. On the other hand, if the items are too general, the charter will not be as dynamic a document. So the best thing is to look for clusters of communication of similar types (e.g. monthly budget reports).

- The process should normally be facilitated by an external facilitator. This will allow the team leader to take part and express personal views more freely.

- In advance of the communication charter session, the team leader should send out some communication to all the team setting out the reasons for the whole process. Extracts from the text of this tool can be used for this purpose.

- If it is more convenient, team members could be briefed and asked to work on their own between meetings to identify their different types of communication (step 7 in the 'How it works' section above). They can then bring the results back to a second session at a later date.

continued overleaf

Facilitation tips continued

- The main emphasis in the communication charter exercise is on internal communications within the team. Make sure the focus stays on this and does not get diverted into other aspects of communication. Consideration could be given to running another similar session to consider communications with other stakeholders at a later date.

- One further step to this exercise could be the preparation of a team communication mission statement, e.g. 'The emergency-response team maintains open and transparent communication among team members on all issues that affect the whole team.' This kind of mission statement could be posted in a position where it is a reminder to everyone who passes through the office.

- Either at the point when the charter is completed, or at the point when the team agrees on a mission statement for communication, the individual members of the team could each make a personal statement expressing their commitment to the team's charter or to the mission statement.

Handout 4a: Links to the ten criteria for trust

Criteria	Definition	Impact of communication charter
Openness with information	Trust based on the observation that other team members share information important to the team proactively and clearly	The creation of a communication charter builds trust by providing an agreed and structured framework for communication within the team, thus enhancing the relevance and effectiveness of all forms of communication.
Integrity	Trust based on the observation that other team members maintain promises, are team-orientated, and behave towards me in accordance with a moral code	A lack of appropriate communication often means that people do not know whether their colleagues have fulfilled their commitments or not. In the absence of information it is easy to assume the worst. The communication charter should help to ensure that people are properly informed and that these suspicions do not arise unnecessarily.
Reciprocity	Trust based on the observation that other group members are trusting and co-operative towards me	Failure to share information appropriately sends out a signal of mistrust. This may not be intentional. It may be due to other factors such as the pressure of work, but it still gives that signal. Once this kind of signal is given, trust levels may be reduced. If this happens, other members of the team may respond accordingly and a downward spiral of trust becomes inevitable.
Inclusion	Trust based on the observation that other team members actively include me in their social and work activities	The communication charter should establish ground rules for sharing information and ideas so that people don't feel left out. This can be particularly important where there are perceived differences of power and the danger of cliques forming, for example among national team members or international team members.

Handout 4b: Communication Charter Example

From whom?	To whom?	Topic/issue?	Method?	Priority?	When?
Team leader	All direct reports	Key decision taken and implications	Telephone call followed up by email	High	When decision is reached
All field staff	Team leader	Situation report	Scheduled telephone call	Medium	Weekly
All field staff	Team leader	Situation report	Written report attached to email	High	By the 3rd of each month
Human resources	All team members	List of new recruits and details of roles and deployment	Online or physical bulletin board Email to those who will be working with them	Low	Before they start
Head of finance	All budget holders	Monthly report of expenditure against budget	Fax and email	Medium	End of first week of following month
Functional heads	Direct reports	Personal support and check on well-being	One-to-one meetings or phone calls	High	At least monthly
Ann Smith	Marwa Hussein	Details of supplies ordered from local supplier	Email	Low	When ready
All managers	Their direct reports	Feedback and objective-setting	One-to-one meetings	High	Monthly
Team leader	All team members	Progress and setbacks	Leader's blog online	Low	Weekly update
Team leader	Team members with most contact with local people	Seeking feedback about help requested by local community	Personal phone calls	Medium	When required
Team leader	Senior managers	Plans for next stage of response	Meeting of senior managers	High	Monthly
Functional head or geographical team leader	IT staff member	Request for additional IT facilities	Phone call followed up by email	Low	As and when identified
Local manager	All team members	Invitation to picnic in the desert	Intranet	Low	A week in advance
Team leader	All team members	Update on funding provisions	Team meeting Cascade through team briefings	Medium	Monthly
Security officer	All team members	Update on security situation	Email	High	As and when required
Logistics manager	All drivers	Revised arrangements for fuelling vehicles	Email with read receipt or individual letters	High	Prior to implementation
Anyone	All team members	Request for a lift into the capital	Intranet	Low	When required

Handout 4c: Communication Media

Item	Advantages	Disadvantages	Suitable content
Team meetings	Face-to-face so body language and high-context communication can be more easily interpreted Opportunities for questions and discussions so that items can be clarified Everyone hears the same information at the same time Major decisions can be recorded People feel involved	Time-consuming Low confidentiality Difficult for people who are geographically separated Reluctance of some to speak up in meetings Open conflicts can arise which are difficult to settle	Co-ordinating conversations Communicating decisions Planning activities Collecting different views and opinions Information updates
Scheduled one-to-one meetings	Face-to-face so body language and high-context communication can be more easily interpreted Opportunities for questions and discussions so that items can be clarified Confidentiality Potential for immediate resolution of differences Gaining agreement Developing personal relationships Less chance of loss of face than in public meetings	Exclusive rather than inclusive – may breed suspicion Reluctance of people to disagree openly with seniors Difficult for people who are geographically separated	Feedback Performance appraisal Personal problems Disciplinary issues Obtaining specific/specialist views and opinions Co-ordinating conversations Planning activities Specific issue discussions
Telephone conversations	Opportunities for discussion and exchange of views Voice enables some interpretation of mood and high-context communication Immediate resolution of differences Gaining agreement Sense of being valued Items can be 'saved up' for the conversation Fast	No record of conversation or details given Cannot observe body language Other person may not be available	Quick progress-reporting Quick positive feedback Keeping up-to-date Resolution of day-to-day issues Making arrangements and plans Providing personal contact and support Maintaining relationships at a distance
Fax	Fast delivery Can use where hard copy only is available Delivery receipts available Can 'broadcast' to lots of people at the same time Recipient can receive later if not present Can go straight into recipient's computer without printing out	Lack of confidentiality Easily lost after delivery Slow for large documents Cannot print double-sided Recipient out of paper Cost of printing and paper Separate line, or blocks phone line	Draft reports for comment Copies of important documents Annotated documents Pictures/photographs/maps etc. Printed materials

Group Two • Tool 4: Communication charter • Handout 4c

Group Two • Tool 4: Communication charter • Handout 4c

Item	Advantages	Disadvantages	Suitable content
Letters	Strongest form of record for keeping Confidential Everyone can receive letters – no need for special equipment etc.	Slow delivery May get lost Postage costs	Contracts etc. which require signatures Official documents
Emails	Quick to prepare Immediate delivery Will wait until recipient is available to read Audit trail of who said what Can 'broadcast' to lots of people at the same time Easy reply and forward facilities Read receipts may be available	Lack of confidentiality Easy to include wrong addressees by mistake Important emails may get swamped out by irrelevant ones Takes time to work through each day Too easy to include 'everyone' – lack of thought about who really needs the information Email boxes get clogged up with irrelevant emails No body language – messages are easily misinterpreted especially across cultural boundaries	Rapid distribution of information to a group of people Making arrangements where the phone is not available Leaving messages for people Asking simple questions and seeking responses
Notice boards	Frequent visual reminder of important notices Can be eye-catching	People at a distance may not have access to the notice board Quickly gets out of date – needs regular maintenance Familiarity may mean people do not bother to read the notices	Displaying relevant extracts of documents/newspapers etc. for all to see Notices regarding social or learning events Exchange requests e.g. seeking lift into town Posters and pictures
SMS (text) messages	Very quick to prepare and send Immediate delivery Will wait until the recipient wants to read Easy reply	Often involves 'shorthand' that can be misinterpreted No record of transmissions	Rapid distribution of information directly to one person and possibly to a group

Tool 5: Aligning working practices

Learning objectives

The purpose of this tool is to:

- bring to the surface the underlying assumptions of team members about how they expect to work together;

- identify differences in assumptions between team members, including the team leaders, especially taking into account differences arising from the diverse backgrounds and experiences of team members (e.g. cultural and gender differences);

- negotiate early agreement on the way team members will work together, and build commitment for this common approach.

Overview

This tool helps team leaders work with their team to agree on some of the ground rules about how team members will work together. Extensive interviews with staff from different agencies have indicated that a participative approach to these issues is most effective. Teams are expected to abide by ground rules, and imposed solutions are less likely to be accepted and more likely to be resisted.

Research shows that successful teams, especially successful multi-cultural teams, take time in the early days to establish ground rules about how they will work together. People from different cultural backgrounds bring different assumptions about how teams operate. If these differences remain unresolved, they lead to intractable problems later in the life of the team. Trust quickly evaporates. The tendency of all new teams, especially those dominated by people from Western cultures, is to start work quickly and focus on the immediate task issues. However, time devoted to agreeing these ground rules represents a very good investment for the team. It will substantially enhance the team's ability to deliver results for the beneficiaries in an effective and efficient manner.

Some examples of the sorts of issues about which assumptions or perceptions differ are:

- How will we design and conduct our meetings?

- How will we make decisions together?

- How will we maximise learning opportunities for team members?

- How will we give feedback to each other?

- What responsibility do the team leader and other team members have for the well-being of team colleagues?

- How will we evaluate our performance together?

- How will conflicts be resolved?

- How will work be co-ordinated – through a command-and-control approach with instructions being issued from above, or through bi-lateral liaison between team members? Will this change with different phases of the work?

The team leader may have to clarify and explain any constraints imposed from outside the team. However, the more freedom the team members can be given to arrive at the best solution for themselves, the better.

Group Two • Tool 5: Aligning working practices

The ECB Trust index identifies the need to align working practices within emergency-response teams (in the Alignment and Cultural factors sections). Alignment of working practices, for example, appears as factor 3 in the Alignment section (page 28). It reads: 'Team members are involved in discussing and agreeing key team processes (e.g. how meetings should be conducted and how conflicts should be resolved)'. If the emergency-response team has used the Trust Index and achieved a negative score for this factor, using this tool is an appropriate way of addressing the problem. It is suggested below that any agreements reached about working practices should be reviewed from time to time. Regular review could also help scores on factor 7 in the Alignment section on page 29 ('Team sessions are held where team performance is reviewed and improvements made as needed').

This tool should be used as soon as possible after the onset of an emergency and in the early stages of a team's life cycle. In the very early chaotic days of a rapid-onset emergency it may be impossible to find the time for the team to work on these issues, so it may be necessary for the leader to adopt a very strong and directive leadership style. Once the immediate life-saving phase is over, this tool should be used to align team members behind a common set of assumptions about the way the team will work together.

Session plan

Overall time required	1 hour and 30 minutes (NB Add 15 minutes if using a warm-up exercise as well)
Group size	6–8 people who work closely together or whose roles make them inter-dependent
Level of facilitation required	High
Relevant Trust Index items	Alignment Cultural
Resources required	Copies of the ten criteria for trust Copies of Handout 5a: Links to the ten criteria for trust Copies of Handout 5b: Working Together: Cultural Values Checklist Multiple flip-charts (ten if possible) with questions and scales from the Cultural Values Checklist (Handout 5b) written on them (see point 2 in 'How it works') Different colour pens (one for each nationality)

How it works

This tool is best used in small groups where the team members are inter-dependent in terms of the work they do. If necessary the process could usefully be repeated in functional or geographical teams. The Cultural Values Checklist (in Handout 5b) could be completed by email or other means of communication before a team meeting, but it will be necessary for the team to meet together face-to-face to understand the results and negotiate agreements.

1.   Where time allows, you should ideally use an ice-breaker as a warm-up exercise in order to minimise barriers to sharing opinions and perspectives.

2. Introduce the objectives of the session. Distribute Handout 5b and ask everyone to complete the Cultural Values Checklist (NB the checklist, with instructions for completing it, is part of Handout 5b and takes about five minutes). Before or while this is taking place, stick the pre-written pieces of flip-chart paper with questions and scales from the Cultural Values Checklist around the room. Place the scale roughly in the middle of each piece of paper.

3. Then ask each person to plot their scores on each piece of flip-chart paper. Each person marks twice on each scale. One score (an 'X') is for what they would like the situation to be. It goes above the line. The second (a small circle) is what they believe the actual situation to be currently. This goes below the line. Get each nationality represented in the team to use a different colour pen to mark their responses.

4. Once all the team members have plotted their responses on the flip-charts, ask team members to visit each of the ten flip-charts and discuss the differences they see and why they have put their crosses and circles in similar or different places. Encourage them to tell stories about things that have worked well in their experience and things that have not worked. Distibute Handout 5a and refer to the trust criteria to reinforce or draw out any issues in the stories or points made in the discussion about the impact of different assumptions.

5. Now help the group negotiate and agree ways of working. Ask the group to discuss in turn each of the questions in Handout 5b (or any other relevant questions about team working practices), bearing in mind the different approaches revealed by the questionnaire.

6. For each item ask them to negotiate an agreement about how they will work together in the future in a way that all can live with and respect. Get them to record their agreement in any way which seems simple and practical. An example may be: 'We agree that for important decisions we will conduct a round-table to get everybody's opinion before making a decision'.

Facilitation tips

- If there are constraints from outside that may limit the freedom of the group to choose their own ways of working together, these should be made clear in advance.

- For the process to be effective, it is important that the team leader allows the group some freedom to work out their own ways of working together. If the group is instructed as to how these things should be done, the value of this session will be greatly reduced.

- In steps 4 and 5 of 'How it works', if there seems to be a high degree of agreement reflected in the scoring, the facilitator can ask the group for practical suggestions (including processes and behaviours) as to how to achieve their preferred ways of working.

continued overleaf

Facilitation tips continued

- Where there are very different responses on a particular question, it may be necessary for the facilitator to explore the thinking or rationale behind each diverse working preference, including the advantages that it may bring to the group. This will provide opportunities for the group to find creative and co-operative responses to the differences revealed. Whether the final decision is made by the team leader or by team consensus may depend on the cultural or organisational context in which the team is operating. However, enabling clarity of different preferences and opinions (particularly if reflected and referred to in the final decision) is likely to be good for building trust within the team.

- Remember that there will be some contexts where making a simple ground rule for behaving may not be possible due to the very different needs of group members. Here it is still useful to make a more general agreement such as 'We agree to respect the different preferences of individual group members about how to give feedback'.

- Choose a setting that is not formal and is preferably away from where normal business meetings take place. It is important to create the impression that this session is something important and different from normal day-to-day work.

- The process should normally be facilitated by the team leader, but the team leader may choose to ask another team member or even an outsider to help. This will allow the team leader to take part and express personal views more freely.

- In advance of the session where the team will work on aligning working practices, the team leader should send out some communication to all the team, setting out the reasons for the whole process. Extracts from the text of this tool would be useful in preparing this communication.

Handout 5a: Links to the ten criteria for trust

Criteria	Definition	Impact of aligning working practices
Competence	Trust based on a perception that team members are competent, and so will not let me down	Perceptions about other people's competence will be partly determined by the way they work. People from different cultures may have different priorities even within their own managerial or technical area. For example, managers who use a participative style may be seen as highly competent by some people, but as indecisive and weak by others.
Compatibility	Trust based on background, values, approaches, interests, and objectives held in common	Sometimes team members work towards different agendas. Sometimes people have different assumptions about the right way of working within the team. They may behave differently from how other team members do. If these things begin to happen, it is likely that the team will fragment into 'cliques' of like-minded people and distrust will grow between the cliques.
Predictability	Trust based on the observation that the behaviour of team members is consistent over time and in different contexts	Each individual's assumptions about the appropriate way to work within a team will determine the way they actually behave in the team context. Assumptions which are not recognised or understood by other team members will make the related behaviours difficult to understand. Trust becomes more difficult if these differences are not brought to the surface and resolved.

Handout 5b: Working Together – Cultural Values Checklist

Purpose

The purpose of this exercise is to encourage you to think about *how* you work together so that you can be effective as a team. Different people, especially if they are from different national cultures, often have divergent expectations about how things should be handled in a team situation. This is an opportunity to discuss these potential differences and agree in advance how you are going to work together.

Task

Your task during this session is to discuss and agree with each other the answers to the following questions for your team:

- How will we design and conduct our meetings?
- How will we make decisions together?
- How will we maximise learning opportunities for team members?
- How will we give feedback to each other?
- What responsibility do the team leader and other team members have for the well-being of team colleagues?
- How will we evaluate our performance together?
- How will conflicts be resolved?
- How will work be co-ordinated – through a command-and-control approach with instructions being issued from above, or through bi-lateral liaison between team members? Will this change with different phases of the work?

BEFORE discussing these questions, however, each person should individually complete the Cultural Values Checklist overleaf, the results of which will inform your discussion.

Instructions

1. Take five minutes to work on your own to fill in the Cultural Values Checklist overleaf, in the manner described below.
2. Working as a group, chart the six individual results for each of the ten questions in the checklist on a flip-chart to see where there are important similarities and differences.
3. Now discuss each of the above questions in turn. Keep in mind the different approaches revealed by the checklist. Try to reach agreement about how you will operate together for future activities.

The Cultural Values Checklist overleaf consists of ten issues, each with descriptions of two opposite approaches at either end of a scale. Please mark the scale with a cross where you personally would like the approach to be, and with a circle where you think it actually is in the team at the moment. For example:

For effective interaction the team should first create a set of ground rules and stick to them.			Effective ground rules will develop through relationships in the team.		
1	2 ⬭ 3	4	5 ✗ 6	7	

If your personal belief and preference is that effective ground rules will develop through relationships, mark the *cross* towards the right-hand end of the scale. If you perceive that actually, within the team in general, and perhaps among the leadership in particular, there is an understanding that creating a set of ground rules from the start will be more effective, mark the *circle* near the left-hand end of the scale.

Cultural Values Checklist

1	For effective interaction the team should first create a set of ground rules and stick to them.			Effective ground rules will develop through relationships in the team.		
	1	2	3	4	5	6	7

2	Roles within the team should be clearly identified at the start of each session.			Team members should adopt the roles they feel comfortable with as things emerge in each session.		
	1	2	3	4	5	6	7

3	The team leader should resolve differences of opinion.			The whole team must reach consensus before moving on.		
	1	2	3	4	5	6	7

4	Expressing strong emotions is inappropriate in the workplace and on this programme.			Expressing all feelings openly and honestly is the only basis for a working relationship.		
	1	2	3	4	5	6	7

5	It takes a long time to get to know someone before you are able to work well together.			You don't need to know people well in order to work effectively with them.		
	1	2	3	4	5	6	7

6	High performance is reached by finishing one thing at a time.			High performance is reached by working on many aspects of the broad picture at the same time.		
	1	2	3	4	5	6	7

7	Effective teamwork comes from highlighting and working with differences.			Effective teamwork comes from highlighting and working with similarities.		
	1	2	3	4	5	6	7

8	One should only say things that are relevant and that are carefully thought through.			Talking about things that simply come to mind can lead to interesting ideas and greater creativity.		
	1	2	3	4	5	6	7

9	Each team member is responsible for making their own contribution to the efforts of the team.			There is a shared responsibility to ensure that all team members have an opportunity to make their contributions.		
	1	2	3	4	5	6	7

10	Both appreciation of and dissatisfaction with other peoples' behaviour should be pointed out directly to them.			Appreciation of and discomfort with other peoples' behaviour is best expressed in subtle and indirect ways.		
	1	2	3	4	5	6	7

Tool 6: Email activity

Learning objectives

The purpose of this tool is to:

- build trust through encouraging a discussion about different communication styles that may exist within the team, and how to reconcile them;

- accelerate awareness of differences in communication styles relating to cultural diversity within the team;

- show how a mis-match in focus (too much or too little relationship/task focus) can lead to a breakdown in trust between different members of the team;

- show how differences in communication styles relating to cultural diversity can affect levels of trust when communicating at a distance.

Overview

The email activity is an apparently simple process in which team members write an email to a colleague they have been communicating with at a distance but have not yet met. The email can be written from two different perspectives – from a national to an international member of staff or vice-versa. Both perspectives share a context in which the colleague is perceived to have failed to respond appropriately, and initiating a feedback process is required. When writing the email, participants are forced to deal with a dilemma. Do they focus on the task and give the person straight feedback (but risk damaging a new and potentially important relationship) or focus on maintaining good relations (but risk not getting through to the person that a change in behaviour is expected)? People in the group explore how they each deal with this dilemma. The activity raises awareness of the logic behind different styles of response to this dilemma. It helps the team find best practices and builds trust by reconciling approaches to communication in pressure situations.

The activity takes the team through one example of a negotiated set of best practices. In this case it is how to set the right tone in managing the process of feedback. In emergency-response efforts this aspect requires immediate shared understanding of how team members prefer to handle this delicate issue, since the international staff are likely to come from lower-context cultures than the local/national staff.

The email activity helps a team in the early stages of forming to address differences in communication style.

Since openness with information is a key criteria in low-context cultures, low-context writers see high-context communication as too fuzzy and too lacking in transparency to trust. In contrast, high-context writers see the low-context writers as overly direct and insensitive to relationships. They give feedback in a more subtle way that 'saves face'. (Goodwill and inclusion are more important criteria in high-context cultures.)

Session plan

Overall time required	1 hour and 15 minutes (NB The activity can be split between two meetings if appropriate)
Group size	10 +
Level of facilitation required	High
Relevant Trust Index items	Cultural factors: high-/low-context communication styles Alignment
Resources required	Copies of the ten criteria for trust for facilitator reference
	Copies of Handout 6a: Links to the ten criteria for trust
	Copies of Handout 6b: The Email Message (National Perspective)
	Copies of Handout 6c: The Email Message (International Perspective)
	Copies of Handout 6d: Email Analysis
	Copies of Handout 6e: Cultural Differences in Communication Style
	Paper-clips or one stapler per group
	One calculator per group (for working out average scores)

How it works

1. Introduce the objectives of the session and the ten criteria for trust. Distribute Handouts 6b and 6c (The Email Message). Give the National Perspective version (Handout 6b) to the national members of the team and the International Perspective version (Handout 6c) to team members from other countries.

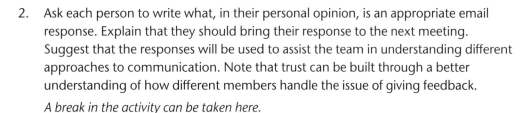

2. Ask each person to write what, in their personal opinion, is an appropriate email response. Explain that they should bring their response to the next meeting. Suggest that the responses will be used to assist the team in understanding different approaches to communication. Note that trust can be built through a better understanding of how different members handle the issue of giving feedback.

   A break in the activity can be taken here.

   If there is to be a break, request team members not to discuss the exercise between now and the next meeting.

3. Now, or at the next session, mention that communication is irreversible – that what is said remains said, and what is written in an email not only remains written but also remains on record.

4. Distribute Handout 6e. It introduces some basic differences between low-context and high-context styles of communication. Ask individuals about their own national cultures and the degree to which they are low- or high-context, and how this may reveal itself in behaviours. Draw on the personal experiences of the team members with high-/low-context breakdowns.

5. Now split the participants into groups of 5–7 people. If possible put the national staff and staff from other countries in separate groups.

6. Assign each group a letter (A, B, or C) or ask them to think of a name for their group. Then, ask participants to mark their completed email sheet with an A, B, or C , or to put their group name in the top left corner.

7. Give the group A emails to group B, group B emails to group C, and group C emails to group A.

8. Distribute Handout 6d: Email Analysis to each group. Ask them to do the following:
    - attach an Email Analysis sheet to each email (back to back) with the stapler or paper-clips provided;
    - read each email individually in silence;
    - complete the analysis by doing the following three things:
        - write their name (first name plus initial of surname, e.g. Mario R.) in the column marked 'Assessor's Name'
        - give their personal reaction rating to the attached email by circling one of the faces in the emotional reaction column – i.e. if they would react positively (happy face), negatively (unhappy face), or neutrally (neutral face).
        - give their low-/high-context rating for that email using the Email Feedback Criteria at the bottom of the page.

    Mention again that low scores, e.g. 2, 3, 4 would mean that, in their opinion, the email is low-context. Higher scores, e.g. 7, 8, 9 would mean that, in their opinion, the email is high-context. Explain that, when a group member has completed these three things, they should pass the email to the person on their *left*. Continue until each group member has read and scored each email. Invite the group to discuss the emails and attempt to reach a consensus on *one* email which best combines the need for *clarity* with the need to *preserve relationships* in handling this task. Put an asterisk (*) in the top left corner of that email.

9. Now ask each person in the group to take one email and calculate the average scores for the emotional reaction (faces) and for the average low-/high-context rating and enter the results in the appropriate spaces in the row marked 'Results'.

10. Arrange for all emails to be handed back to the original writers together with the attached scoring sheet. Give people a few seconds to look at their scores. They will see how 5–7 other people have interpreted their message.

Another break in the activity can be taken here.

11. Now (or at the next session) ask everyone to stand up with their emails and scores in their hand and ask them to form a semi-circle with the very low-context average scores at one end and the very high-context average scores at the other.

12. Ask people at the low-context end if they would share what their intention was in writing the email in this way and ask them if they would mind if you (the facilitator) read it for everyone to hear. Facilitate a discussion of the advantages and disadvantages of communicating in this style. Then choose an email from the high-context end of the semi-circle. Repeat.

13. Now call out numbers representing the emotional reaction range, asking people to sit down when they hear theirs called out. Start with the highest (+2 smiley faces or above) and go down the range to –2 and below. As facilitator, note which people sit down first (often very high-context ones). The low-context ones often sit down last.

14. Then, when they are all seated, identify people who have an email with the asterisks (*) to read out their email. Find out how they have succeeded in reconciling a 'clarity' with a 'relationship' focus. Note that the asterisked emails are often just on the higher-context side of 5 (i.e. with an average low-/high-context score of between 5 and 7). This becomes the group benchmark for handling this situation.

15. Conclude the exercise by saying something like: 'We have explored in the team which communication styles we find too direct and those which are too indirect. The asterisks give us an indication of which styles work for most of us.' Distribute Handout 6a outlining the criteria for trust which are reinforced by the email activity.

Facilitation tips

- Arrange to have a stapler and a calculator on each table.

- If you wish to split the activity between two meetings, you can complete items 1 and 2 from the list under 'How it works', and have them prepare their draft emails before they come back for the next meeting.

- Make sure you understand and can summarise the differences between high-context and low-context cultures. Use these terms during the session to get people used to them and to create a common language to talk about these issues.

- Until you are familiar with the whole process, take the activity step by step and have the 'How it works' section handy to refer to as you work your way through the process.

- Do not assume that staff from other countries (international staff) will respond to the activity in a low-context style and national staff in a high-context style. There will be a mix based on personal style, experience, and professional background. Some people will consciously adapt their style to their perception of the needs and preferences of others.

- If you do not have a mix of national and international staff in your group, divide the group into two and distribute Handout 6b to one half and Handout 6c to the other half.

- With smaller groups a mix of email scenarios can be given out, and the email analysis can take place in one group only. Note that the writer of the email is not required to analyse his or her own email.

- This exercise is designed to support awareness and an interest in change. It can create the commitment to change which is necessary for the team leader to develop ground rules for communicating in the team.

Handout 6a: Links to the ten criteria for trust

Criteria	Definition	Impact of email activity
Openness with information	Trust based on the observation that other team members share information important to the team proactively and clearly	This activity highlights how misunderstandings can arise due to different communication styles. People with low-context styles may feel that high-context communication is not clear, and so may suspect the motives of the writer.
Reciprocity	Trust based on the observation that other team members are trusting and co-operative towards me	Misunderstandings due to different communication styles can lead to questions or doubts about the motives and intentions of other people. This is especially true where the communication is only through emails. Mistrust can escalate as each person begins to believe that the other does not trust them.
Goodwill	Trust based on the belief that other team members are concerned about my overall welfare	People from high-context cultures will look for signals that other people are concerned about their welfare. People from low-context cultures provide few such signals, especially in emails. This may lead those from high-context cultures to believe that those from low-context cultures are not interested in them or in their welfare. This can contribute to mistrust.
Inclusion	Trust based on the observation that other team members actively include me in their social and work activities	People from high-context cultures look for signals that they are being included in discussions and/or exchanges of written communication. The lack of response to previous communications portrayed in the scenarios used for this activity suggests that the parties may feel excluded – leading again to mistrust.

Handout 6b: The Email Message (National Perspective)

You are working in an emergency-team project in your own country with colleagues from a mixture of national cultural backgrounds. Some of the staff from other countries are preparing to enter the emergency zone next week. Others are national staff who have been working on the ground in the emergency zone for the past five days. At the moment, these two groups are limited to email communciation The language for communicating with fellow team-members is English.

You are very dissatisfied with the way one colleague from another country is managing this project. This person does not seem to understand that some initial arrangements and practices to handle the emergency are already in place and working. This particular colleague has ignored the fact that you have already reported setting up these workable local arrangements. The person insists that everything needs to be organised from scratch. It is clear that you need to signal your dissatisfaction and attempt to change their attitude. It is also clear that you need to do something about this situation now. If nothing changes, the unity of purpose and co-ordination of activities required to respond effectively to the emergency will be compromised. For example, there may be an unnecessary duplication of structures and procedures.

Note that the relationship with this person is of strategic importance to you and the project. Although you have had email and telephone calls with this person, you have not met the person face-to-face. Both of you are at the same level of responsibility in the team.

Write a short email in English to initiate the feedback process. Write your email in the box below.

PLEASE WRITE CLEARLY

To	
From	
CC	
BCC	
Subject	
Message	

Handout 6c: The Email Message (International Perspective)

You are working as one of the international members in an emergency-response team with colleagues from a mixture of national cultural backgrounds. You and some of the staff are preparing to enter the emergency zone for an assessment next week. There is a group of national staff who have been working in the zone for the past five days. At the moment, you are limited to email communication. The language for communication with fellow team-members is English.

You are very dissatisfied with the approach being used by your key national counterpart to manage this project. This person has not responded to your requests to provide initial input for an on-the-ground assessment necessary to create a plan for staffing levels. All you get back are reports on what has already been done. You feel cut out and are concerned that crucial issues are not being carefully considered. Taking initiative is fine but co-ordination of activities is essential.

It is clear that you need to signal your dissatisfaction and achieve a change in this person's attitude. It is also clear that you need to do something about this situation now. If nothing changes, the unity of purpose and co-ordination of activities required to respond effectively to the emergency will be compromised.

Note that the relationship with this person is of strategic importance to you and the project. Although you have had email and telephone calls with this person, you haven't met the person face-to-face. You are at the same level of responsibility in the team.

Write a short email in English to initiate the feedback process. Write your email in the box below.

PLEASE WRITE CLEARLY

To	
From	
CC	
BCC	
Subject	
Message	

Handout 6d: Email Analysis

In your sub-group, each of you should assess the emails from another group. Put your name under 'Assessor's Name'. Read one email and fill in the scorecard below. Then pass the email to the next person in the group until each member of the group has scored all of the emails.

There are two separate scores:

- Your emotional reaction if you had personally received this email – happy, neutral, or sad (☺ ☺ ☹)
- Your personal rating from 1–10 of the low-/high-context orientation of the email (1= very low context; 10 = very high context). The criteria for your assessment are at the bottom of the page.

Email scorecard

Assessor's Name	Emotional Reaction	Low-Context								High-Context
	☺ ☺ ☹	1	2	3	4	5	6	7	8	9 10
	☺ ☺ ☹	1	2	3	4	5	6	7	8	9 10
	☺ ☺ ☹	1	2	3	4	5	6	7	8	9 10
	☺ ☺ ☹	1	2	3	4	5	6	7	8	9 10
	☺ ☺ ☹	1	2	3	4	5	6	7	8	9 10
	☺ ☺ ☹	1	2	3	4	5	6	7	8	9 10
	☺ ☺ ☹	1	2	3	4	5	6	7	8	9 10
Now (if you are the final assessor)	Work out the emotional reaction scores. For each ☺ give one point (+1) For each ☹ deduct one point (-1) Ignore all ☺ (0)	Add up the total high-/low-context rating scores above and divide by the number of people who analysed the email. This gives the average high-/low-context rating.								
RESULTS	**Emotional Reaction score?**	**Average Low/High score?**								

Email Feedback Criteria

Low context	High context
I/you focus	We/us focus
Starts with task	Starts with relationship
Feedback in message	Feedback deferred to face-to-face or phone
Direct and explicit – spells it out	Indirect and implicit – must read between the lines
Clarity is primary	Saving face is primary

Handout 6e: Cultural Differences in Communication Style

How do cultural differences in communication style impact on your team? 'Low-context' team members learn from their national cultural background that effective communication is about 'saying what you mean and meaning what you say'. They tend to rely on written communication (such as minutes of meetings, agendas, contracts) to 'spell out' meaning. Trust is built quickly by being clear and focusing on the task. North Americans, Australasians, and Northern Europeans tend to be brought up to have a low-context approach to communication.

'High-context' team members value the ability of the sensitive listener who can 'read between the lines', and understand the damage done to relationships by straight talking. They tend to avoid writing and rely on broad spoken agreements. Trust is built slowly by protecting face and focusing on relationship. South and South-East Asians, Africans, Middle-Easterners, South Americans, as well as Southern Europeans tend to have a higher-context approach.

Look at the following behaviours and beliefs connected to low- and high-context work environments, and consider whether you have such cultural differences in your team.

Low-context	High-context
Be direct and task-focused	Be indirect and relationship-focused
Be explicit and specific	Communicate between the lines or through non-verbal means
Write things down and 'spell things out'	Keep things oral
Give feedback as soon as possible, in a direct manner	Give feedback indirectly, and at the right time in order to save face
Believe that trust in your competence leads to deeper levels of relationships, so begin with the task	Believe that deeper levels of personal trust are required for tasks to be carried out effectively, so begin with relationship-building
Believe that being clear shows respect	Believe that sensitivity about saving face shows respect

A combination of both low-context and high-context cultural preferences can lead to great synergies in nurturing trust in international teams where trust is fragile. Combining 'clarity' (low-context) with 'rapport' (high-context) is critical for building a productive working atmosphere. However, when these differences are not recognised and respected, the result can be the opposite. Low-context directness can be perceived as 'insensitivity' and a high-context indirectness can be considered as 'time-wasting'.

Tool 7: Trust tips for team leaders

Learning objectives

The purpose of this tool is to:

- highlight some key behaviours and activities that team leaders can use to promote trust within their teams.

Overview

This tool presents a series of tips that individual leaders can use as a checklist of ideas for promoting trust within the team. The tips are categorised under the ten criteria for trust. The ideas are drawn from a number of sources relevant to the emergency-response team situation; many of the ideas come from interviews that were carried out as part of the 'Culture of Trust' project with experienced field staff in a number of agencies.

This tool could be incorporated into agencies' existing leadership-development activities that take place outside the context of any particular emergency. It can also be used by the team leaders at any stage during the life of a team to help plan trust-building behaviours and activities. It can be used either as the leader reflects on their own leadership behaviours, or as a basis for a coaching process for the leader. Many people believe that the style of leadership required during the very early days of a rapid-onset emergency will, of necessity, be very directive in order to give a clear lead to make things happen in a confused situation. As soon as this initial phase is over, however, a more participative style will be more appropriate, and this list of trust tips will be particularly relevant at that time in helping leaders to 'change gear' and settle into a more sustainable approach to the leadership role.

The Trust Index helps teams to assess the factors that will make trust easier or more difficult in the emergency-response team in their particular situations. *This* tool will help to address low scores for any of the dimensions contained in the Leadership section of that Index (page 26).

This tool can be used by any emergency-response team member who has line responsibility for managing other people.

How it works

A number of trust tips for leaders are set out in Handout 7a, grouped according to the ten criteria for trust. The first four categories are designed to build 'swift' trust, whilst the remaining six categories will help to build 'deeper' trust. The 'swift' trust criteria include aspects of trust required by, for example, virtual teams with a complex task to achieve. The 'deeper' criteria are relevant when the level of trust needs to increase and to be based around personal relationships.

For each of the ten criteria a definition is given at the start of the relevant section. This is expressed in terms of the needs of individual team members for specific behaviours from other team members. The leader needs to think about all the items at two levels, namely:

1. How can I behave in ways which will build the trust of others in myself as the team leader?
2. How can I model behaviours that build trust between all members of the team?

Handout 7a: Trust Tips for Leaders

Swift Trust – Competence

Definition

Trust based on a perception that team members are competent, and so will not let me down.

1. Take the time to understand the particular skills, knowledge, and capabilities of each team member. Study CVs and background experiences to estimate the particular work each person can do and the contribution they can make.

2. Give due weight to the knowledge and skills of local members of the team, even if they are not so well-defined through formal qualifications. Under-estimating the value that local people can bring to the team will make it difficult to establish trust between the local and non-local members of the team. Knowledge of local circumstances (e.g. geography and geology) and of the local community will often be essential to the whole team's success.

3. Where possible, allow all team members to demonstrate openly their areas of competence to fellow team members through the work they do. Remember that team members from more collectivist cultures (where the interests of the group are emphasised over those of the individual) are less likely to advertise their skills to the rest of the team, for fear of standing out too much from the group, and appearing competitive. So find ways to catalogue and communicate each individual's particular strengths to other team members (e.g. use Tool 10: Time lines on page 114 to enable team members to understand each other's history and experiences).

4. Sometimes it may be necessary to include people in the team whose capabilities are not fully matched to the job they are given to do. In this case make sure that they receive support and have access to the knowledge and skills of others who can help them. Consider establishing a 'buddy' system so that, where necessary, local people can draw on the expertise of international colleagues and vice versa.

5. Implement existing performance-management systems as soon as possible, so that deficiencies in skills and knowledge are identified. Make sure that plans are in place to overcome these deficiencies through coaching, training, or other developmental activities.

6. People recruited in the early days of an emergency may not be well-equipped to contribute in the later phases of the work. In this situation, use your local human-resources function to move people out of the team and replace them with more competent people. Trust will not be built if the leader turns a blind eye to poor performance due to inadequate capabilities.

7. Through your human-resources function, develop a detailed understanding of the local labour market and the skills that are available locally. This will enable you to judge the right balance between local and international employees. Ensure that you employ local staff wherever possible.

Swift Trust – Openness with Information

Definition

Trust based on the observation that other team members share information important to the team proactively and clearly.

1. Arrange a session to establish a communication charter for the senior management team. Encourage other functional and/or geographical teams to do the same.

2. Make sure that everyone is aware of any agency communication protocols.

3. Spend as much time as you can in face-to-face meetings and discussions with team members. Ask open questions and listen carefully to the answers. Encourage the same behaviour from other people.

4. Make sure that all team members are very clear about what outputs you expect from them and when. Use simple, well-structured language to communicate this, particularly to people who do not share your own mother tongue. Remember that people from different cultures may have different ways of understanding time and deadlines.

5. Provide people with feedback on a regular basis and in a culturally sensitive way (e.g. avoid people losing 'face'). It does not help trust within the team if the poor performance or bad behaviours of some individuals is allowed to persist.

6. Develop with your team a simple set of confidentiality criteria that ensures that everyone understands what kinds of things are confidential.

7. If you need to keep important information confidential, explain the reasons to the team members and, if possible, say when you will be able to release the information.

8. Arrange office layouts and communication hardware to ensure that 'silos' or 'cliques' do not develop (in other words, try to stop people getting into cosy and comfortable groups based on work functions or friendships).

9. Remember that different people have different preferences, expectations, and habits concerning *how* to communicate (for example: written or oral; through the literal meaning of the words used, or through reading between the lines and observing body language). Allow for these differences when communicating important messages.

10. Communicate key messages repeatedly and in different ways. Tell stories and recount experiences to illustrate points that you want to get across.

11. Communicate more frequently when things are changing quickly.

12. Take account of cultural sensitivities about communication. Quieter team members still need to communicate but may lack the confidence or feel that it is inappropriate to join in team discussions. Make sure that you allow them the opportunity in team discussions and encourage them to give their views.

13. Use group and pair work to secure greater participation rather than assuming that brainstorming will work.

14. Make sure that you share information equally between all team members. Do not favour some team members over others. Ensure that the method you choose to communicate a message does not discriminate through making it easier for some people to access than others (e.g. using emails when some people do not have access).

Swift Trust – Integrity

Definition

Trust based on the observation that other team members maintain promises, are team-orientated, and behave towards me in accordance with a moral code.

1. Do not promise things that you are not sure you or others can deliver.

2. Remember that people interpret language differently when it comes to commitment (e.g. if you make the statement: 'I will try to speak to headquarters about this before the end of the week', this could be interpreted as an intention or as a promise).

3. Remember that in many cultural contexts an apparent agreement to take on a task may reflect a desire to please the team leader rather than a verbal contract.

4. Keep in mind that your body language may say something different from your spoken words. Some people may read this difference and others may not. You will often be working in cultural contexts where sensitivity to 'between the line' and contextual communication is critical. So ensure that your verbal and body language are compatible.

5. Record all important decisions in writing as soon as possible. Check with those involved to make sure that there is no confusion later on.

6. If you are unable to meet a commitment, or if you have to reverse a decision, make sure that you tell those involved as soon as possible and explain the reasons why.

7. Hold other team members to account for their behaviour and for the commitments they make. Be clear that you have high expectations that they can, and will, meet targets; but do not blame team members for circumstances outside their control (e.g. well-being or lack of it).

8. Treat all team members with dignity and respect at all times.

9. Be clear about the behaviour that you expect from others, and model these behaviours yourself. Criticising others for things you do yourself will be seen as hypocritical.

10. Allow people to see and understand the standards and moral codes that you live by. Openly admit your weaknesses and mistakes. Do not hide them but show that you are ready to learn from them.

Swift Trust – Reciprocity

Definition

Trust based on the observation that other team members are trusting and co-operative towards me.

1. Find areas where you can trust team members and give clear signals that you are prepared to trust them. At first, choose areas where little damage will be done if they break or betray your trust. But remember if there is no risk to you, you are not demonstrating trust! In more relationship-orientated cultures, make clear your own personal vulnerability if the work is not done well.

2. Where your trust is honoured and returned, gradually take greater risks in extending trust to new areas. In this way you should be able to establish a positive spiral of mutual trust.

3. Use specific delegated tasks and responsibilities to extend and build trust gradually. Always balance the need for control with the need to build trust (e.g. delegated authority to spend money).

4. Make it clear through your words as well as your actions that you are ready to trust others, and that you have high expectations that your trust will not be betrayed.

5. Take time to establish rapport and good personal relationships with other members of the team; trust is less likely to be broken where there are personal loyalties involved.

6. If your trust is broken, establish why this happened and what motives were involved. If the breach was not deliberate (e.g. it was through lack of appropriate skills to deal with a situation), show that you forgive the breach and are prepared to continue to trust. Support the individual with coaching or training to reduce the chances of it happening again.

7. Where a breach of trust is deliberate, reduce the trust that you extend to the individual. However, limit the extent of this withdrawal of trust to avoid a negative spiral being established. If possible, find new areas in which to show trust and gradually rebuild mutual trust.

8. Monitor levels of trust within the team, both through your own observation and also using the available tools to measure trust levels. Set up trust-building team activities from time to time.

9. Earn the trust of colleagues in your agency, and particularly the person to whom you report. If you are trusted by them you will be able to influence upwards more easily and obtain the support and resources that your team needs. In turn, this will help your team members to respect and trust you.

10. Ensure that difficult issues that may cause conflict are resolved quickly. Indecision about difficult issues will result in trust seeping away.

11. When differences and conflicts arise, use conflict-resolution techniques to repair damage and re-establish a positive spiral.

12. Remember that in relationship-orientated cultures you can inspire trust when giving feedback by avoiding the singling out of individuals in group meetings, where possible. Be ready to deliver the hardest messages to individuals on a one-to-one basis.

Deeper Trust – Compatibility

Definition

Trust based on background, values, approaches, interests, and objectives held in common.

1. Emergency-response teams will usually contain people who are very different in terms of culture, life experiences, economic status, age etc. As a team leader, your task is to:

   • find and emphasise areas of commonality between them;

   • build respect for the differences and find ways to use these for the benefit of the overall effort.

   These things are best achieved by using a process such as that described in Tool 5: Aligning working practices (page 79).

2. Differences can best be harnessed for the good of the whole team if a sense of common direction and purpose is established. Ensure that all team members understand the values and objectives of the agency they are working for, and then work with the team to establish a common vision and common goals that all the team members can support.

3. Through the recruitment and selection processes, ensure that all team members are open to working with people who are different from them. People who are not open and flexible in this way may need to be removed from the team.

Deeper Trust – Goodwill

Definition

Trust based on the belief that other team members are concerned about my overall welfare.

1. Explicitly indicate that you have considered the impact of the decisions you take on all team members.

2. Put a high priority on the 'hygiene factors' for team members and make sure these are as good as they can be in the circumstances (e.g. food, water, accommodation, facilities for relaxation etc.). Where possible, indicate plans and timings for their improvement over time, as circumstances allow.

3. Similarly, place a high priority on working conditions, and make sure they are as good as they can be under the circumstances (e.g. avoid over-crowded workstations, promote an awareness of stress factors, and work with the team to reduce these). Make sure team members take time off for relaxation. Lead by example!

4. Treat all team members equally and fairly. Do not give preferential treatment to anybody.

5. Get to know team members as individuals, as far as time and circumstances allow. Acknowledge and respond to their personal needs and circumstances (e.g. important family events, the impact of the disaster on them personally, etc.).

6. Put in place arrangements (perhaps through the human-resources department) that ensure that all team members are watched for signs of undue stress, and that those who need it receive individual help and support.

7. Encourage a sense of mutual support and responsibility for each other across the whole team. Communicate this message and demonstrate this behaviour.

8. As far as possible, make sure that people take the time off to which they are entitled. Do not permit a 'hero' culture to develop where there is a spirit of competition to see who can work the longest hours or put up with the worst conditions.

9. Find opportunities to openly value the contributions that individual team members make to the overall effort. Remember, however, that in collectivist cultures, work delegated to an individual may have been completed in a group. Occasionally select trust-building behaviours for special attention and reward.

10. Remember that in more relationship-orientated cultures the amount of one-to-one time you spend with local staff is a sign of your goodwill.

Deeper Trust – Predictability

Definition

Trust based on the observation that the behaviour of team members is consistent over time and in different contexts.

1. Establish clear expectations and guidelines for the team, and for yourself, about those behaviours that are acceptable and those that are not. Then make sure you live within these rules and try to ensure that others do so too. (NB Agencies may already have a code of conduct that can act as a starting point for this.)

2. Do not behave erratically or in an uncontrolled way. It is difficult for others to trust someone whose behaviour they cannot anticipate. This does not mean that your behaviour should always be the same, but rather that it should vary in predictable ways depending on the circumstances.

3. Get to know and begin to understand the personalities and motivations of the key members of your team so you can better predict their behaviour and reactions. As you come to understand them, you will find it easier to understand how you can trust them.

4. Study the cultural differences within the team, and between yourself and other team members. This will help you avoid misunderstandings and mis-communication. It may also help to explain apparent breaches of trust (e.g. in cultures where all property is considered to be held by the community and not by individuals, 'theft' can take on a different significance).

5. Establish a culture of 'no surprises'.

6. Build systems and procedures and make these clear so that people understand how they are meant to be working. Confusion and ambiguity leads to insecurity and conflicts which destroy trust.

Deeper Trust – Well-being

Definition

Trust arising from the feeling that I have nothing to fear from other members of the team.

1. Establish a culture of mutual respect within the team. Demonstrate behaviour that shows respect, and take a strong line against any example of physical or verbal intimidation or bullying of team members.

2. Encourage assertiveness but not aggression.

3. Pay particular attention to the way that women are treated. Do not allow it to become acceptable for male members of the team to 'put down,' belittle, or ignore the contributions of female team members in any way. This can sometimes be done in a subtle, even apparently friendly, way, but should still not be tolerated. From time to time check on how the women members of the team feel about their position within the team.

4. At all costs avoid a 'blame' culture. When things go wrong, put the emphasis on learning and changing things for the future. Ask the team to identify the circumstances that contributed to things going wrong and work on the things they suggest.

5. If you need to reprimand a team member or give them difficult feedback, do so in a one-to-one meeting to avoid loss of face for them. This is particularly important in high-context work environments.

6. If teasing and banter between team members becomes frequent, be careful to ensure that all team members are comfortable with it and feel that they can give as good as they get. If not, then stop the associated behaviour. Make sure that humour is not generated at the expense of individuals or a particular national group.

Deeper Trust – Inclusion

Definition

Trust based on the observation that other group members actively include me in their social and work activities.

1. Demonstrate through your own behaviour that you treat all team members equally and fairly. Expect all senior team members to do the same.

2. Watch out for the formation of 'cliques' or 'silos' within the overall team, especially by the local or the international team members (in other words, try to stop people getting into cosy and comfortable groups based on work functions or friendships). Take action to break down any such barriers (e.g. arrange meetings/social events which cut across silos; change office layouts, etc.).

3. All work and organised social activities should be explicitly inclusive of all team members. However, it is often a relief for individuals to socialise with people from their own culture or with those who share a common mother tongue.

4. Involve people in the decision-making process wherever possible. This does not mean that decisions should normally be taken on a consensus basis, but it does mean that when you take major decisions you have listened to and understood the ideas, opinions, and information that others have to offer.

5. Involve the team in a process that results in agreement on what kinds of information must be communicated to the whole team (see Tool 4: Communication charter on page 70).

6. Consider carefully whom to include in communication. Excluding people can send a negative signal about trust. However, including people who do not need to know can waste their time. Overcome this by being explicit about whom you are including in major communications and why, and give everyone an opportunity to opt in if they wish (see Tool 4: Communication charter on page 70).

7. As soon as work pressures allow, encourage social activities that include all team members. Try to get local team members to take the lead in organising these events, as they will know about the fun things to do locally (e.g. a picnic in the desert or a night under the stars).

8. Ensure that any privileges or perks are kept to a minimum and based on the legitimate needs of the job (e.g. access to vehicles). Try to minimise the 'power distance' between the leaders and the rest of the team. Be aware that separate and superior offices, greater access to vehicles, provision of pre-paid mobile phones, higher quality accommodation, etc. for senior managers, sends a powerful and negative message about inclusion. Go to visit team members where they work; do not always expect them to come to you. Where team members are sharing accommodation provided by the agency, visit team members where they live to demonstrate your interest in their well-being.

9. Consciously seek to make use of the local knowledge and community ties of team members from the local area. Openly recognise this as a major contribution that they can make to the overall effort.

Deeper Trust – Accessibility

Definition

Trust based on the observation that other team members share their true feelings and I can relate to them on a personal level.

1. Be ready to show your feelings and emotions to other team members so that they can know you better. There is no harm in them knowing that you are frustrated on occasions, provided you do not take your frustrations out on them.

2. Remember that there are gender and cultural elements involved in expressing emotions.

3. Followers can draw enthusiasm and motivation from their leader if they are exposed to the leader's energies and emotions. They cannot do this if the leader is distant, cool, or hard to know as a human being.

4. As far as is possible, be accessible to team members both physically and emotionally. Let them see you around whenever possible, and talk with them. It is easier to trust a person that you know.

5. Share your personal hopes and fears freely within the team. Do not feel it is a sign of weakness to let others see that you occasionally need help and support.

6. Involve the team in the creation of a 'vision' that expresses how they can make a real difference to the people affected by the disaster. Refer to it frequently in ways that appeal to people's imagination and values.

Building Trust in Diverse Teams

Tool 8: Elements for team leader 360° reviews

Learning objective

The purpose of this tool is to:

- provide a bank of statements that can easily be inserted into existing 360° review processes to assist team leaders in assessing their contribution toward the building of trust within emergency-response teams.

Overview

The team leader has a central role in creating a culture of trust in their emergency-response team. Understanding and raising awareness of this role, and identifying both strengths and development needs, will be key to team leaders' success and ongoing development.

This tool provides a bank of statements that are specifically anchored to the ten criteria for trust. Agencies will be able to incorporate some or all of these statements into their own 360° review process in order to evaluate the trust dimension of their team leaders and managers.

The items contained in this tool can be used in two distinct ways. First, they can be incorporated into an agency's existing 360° review process. Second, the ECB Trust Index identifies leadership as one of the key factors that enhances or destroys trust within emergency-response teams. So if the emergency-response team has used the Trust Index and achieved a low score for this factor, then the items in this tool can be used to create a 360° questionnaire specifically focused on the leader's trust behaviours. Using these items in a suitable 360° questionnaire and feedback process will enable the team leader to change their own behaviour to promote trust more effectively. It should help to move the score on this dimension in the Trust Index in a positive direction.

Completion of 360° review questionnaires requires respondents to have some knowledge of and experience of working with the team leader. Thus the items in the handout could be used outside the context of a specific emergency, to give a leader feedback as part of their own overall development. This would require people who have worked with the leader in the recent past (line manager, peers, and those directly reporting to the leader) to provide feedback. For example, this could be done appropriately as part of a project review process. Alternatively, the items could be used as part of a 360° process during the life of an emergency-response team, although it would be impractical to do this during the immediate aftermath of a rapid-onset emergency, or too early in the life of the team, as team members might not have sufficient knowledge of the leader's behaviours.

How it works

The statements are listed in Handout 8a. There are five statements for each of the ten criteria for trust, resulting in a total of 50 statements. It should be stressed that it is not intended that all of these statements necessarily be incorporated into an existing 360° questionnaire. Rather, the agency should identify which of the criteria for trust they wish to measure and then select the items they wish to include to assess these criteria. They are listed as statements rather than questions in the expectation that the existing 360° framework includes scales such as strongly agree/agree/disagree/strongly disagree. If necessary the statements can be turned into questions.

Group Three • Tool 8: Elements for team leader 360° reviews

Handout 8a: Items for Inclusion in 360° Leadership Reviews

Criteria	Definition	Items
Competence	Trust based on a perception that team members are competent, and so will not let me down	Is an experienced and effective leader for an emergency-response team Understands the bigger picture and is able to interpret it so that others can make sense of it Is able to deliver high-level results through the work of the team Is knowledgeable about emergency-response work Is someone I would go to for advice and information about our area of work
Openness with Information	Trust based on the observation that other team members share information important to the team proactively and clearly	Exchanges information in a transparent and unambiguous way Readily shares relevant information with all team members Keeps team members informed about important decisions that affect their work Shares important organisational messages with the team Clearly communicates shared goals and objectives to the team
Integrity	Trust based on the observation that other team members maintain promises, are team-orientated, and behave towards me in accordance with a moral code	Keeps promises and commitments Is honest and truthful Does not focus on own success at the expense of the team Behaves ethically Admits mistakes and apologises when appropriate
Reciprocity	Trust based on the observation that other team members are trusting and co-operative towards me	Is ready to accept help and support from team members Trusts team members to get on with the job Depends on team members for own success Ready to learn and encourages feedback from team members Is prepared to take some risks in trusting others
Compatibility	Trust based on background, values, approaches, interests, and objectives held in common	Holds values that I can understand and respect Establishes common approaches to work that we can all follow Emphasises common objectives to co-ordinate the work of team members Works towards common goals rather than own private agenda Achieves buy-in from team members

Criteria	Definition	Items
Goodwill	Trust based on the belief that other team members are concerned about my overall welfare	Is genuinely concerned about my welfare Is helpful towards me Makes every effort to understand my priorities and interests Provides me with support when I need it Recognises when I have achieved something, and rewards my performance
Predictability	Trust based on the observation that the behaviour of team members is consistent over time and in different contexts	Behaves in a rational and dependable way Is reliable Is steady and dependable under pressure Clearly defines roles and responsibilities for the team Provides clear and consistent direction for the team
Well-being	Trust arising from the feeling that I have nothing to fear from other members of the team	Encourages me to speak my mind Is tolerant when divergent or unpopular views are expressed Is not dominating or controlling towards team members Allows for individual initiative and innovation within the team Does not judge me negatively for making genuine mistakes
Inclusion	Trust based on the observation that other team members actively include me in their social and work activities	Listens and responds positively to my ideas and opinions Treats me and other members of the team as equals Creates a strong sense of team spirit Invites team members to contribute to key decisions Shares successes with all team members
Accessibility	Trust based on the observation that other team members share their true feelings and I can relate to them on a personal level	Deals with others in a personal and human fashion Is open about own needs and motives Does not hide own feelings from team members Gets to know team members on a personal basis Creates personal loyalty amongst team members

Tool 9: Treasure hunting

Learning objectives

The purpose of this tool is to:

*   enable people to meet and get to know each other;
*   begin a process which lets all team members appreciate the gifts and qualities that each person brings to the team, and to see the diversity of background, culture, and skills that are available in the team.

Overview

For team members to trust each other, they need to know each other. This tool consists of a fun activity which creates energy and can be used anytime – but is particularly good in the first week as an ice-breaker. For this activity, team members move around the room and talk to fellow team members to find the answers to some questions from anyone they feel might have the answers.

Session plan

Overall time required	50 minutes
Group size	10 +
Level of facilitation required	Low
Relevant Trust Index items	Team composition Alignment
Resources required	Copies of Handout 9a: Links to the ten criteria for trust Copies of Handout 9b: List of Questions for Treasure Hunting

How it works

1. Introduce the exercise with team members standing in a circle. Hand out a list of questions to each participant. (A sample is provided in Handout 9b and the questions can be adapted depending on the composition and needs of the group.)

2. Allow 20 minutes for participants to go around the room and find answers to the questions from anyone they feel may have the answers.

3. Inform them that they must not take more than one piece of information from the same person, and they are not allowed to form groups of more than three people at any one time. This encourages more interaction from different members of the group. Also inform them that they are not allowed to pass on the answer they have received from one person on a specific question to another person (if they are asked the same question).

4. After 20–30 minutes, ask the participants to return to the circle. Go through all the questions and ask participants to raise their hand if they got an answer. Then debrief the activity as follows:

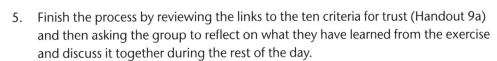

- Who feels that they got a unique or surprising answer?

- Which questions made you feel uncomfortable when you were asking them? Why?

- What did you notice about the process you used to find the answers?

- How many of you were asked the same question constantly? Why do you think this was so?

- Who was asked a question they do not normally get asked? What did that feel like?

5. Finish the process by reviewing the links to the ten criteria for trust (Handout 9a) and then asking the group to reflect on what they have learned from the exercise and discuss it together during the rest of the day.

Facilitation tips

- This exercise is a great way to begin a session, as it encourages participants to go around the room and introduce themselves to each other, and it immediately gets them interested in important diversity questions.

- The exercise is most effective for groups which are diverse in terms of national culture, gender, age, and experience.

- Experience of running this activity suggests that although there is a limited time frame, most questions get answered. Solutions to any challenge exist in the room.

- Some participants note that they get asked the same questions – and this stimulates a conversation around why this is so. For example, participants go to the only African in the room to find out what it was like growing up poor. This stimulates a dialogue about the assumptions we have about how we define poverty and who experiences it.

- Others note that it felt good to be asked a question they don't normally get asked, but to have a good idea on how to handle the situation. This stimulates a conversation about what we miss when we go to the same people for answers and overlook others.

- This exercise highlights how the diversity in the room contributes to a variety of solutions and ideas for change.

- This exercise highlights the different approaches people use to get responses to their questions.

- Note that the questions can be customised to the team that you are working with.

This tool has been reproduced and adapted with the permission of CARE International. It is from *Promoting Gender Equality and Diversity: A CARE Training Curriculum for Facilitators*, Module Three, Managing Diversity, pp.129–30; 157–8 (2005).

Group Four • Tool 9: Treasure hunting

Handout 9a: Links to the ten criteria for trust

Criteria	Definition	Impact of treasure hunting
Competence	Trust based on a perception that team members are competent, and so will not let me down	Treasure hunting uncovers hidden assumptions about who is competent in which areas.
Reciprocity	Trust based on the observation that other team members are trusting and co-operative towards me	Through taking part in these activities team members are to some extent making themselves vulnerable, and they all take this risk together.
Accessibility	Trust based on the observation that other team members share their true feelings and I can relate to them on a personal level	The questions are designed to enable people to find out something about the values and attitudes of other people in the room. This helps other team members to get to know them better on a personal level.

Handout 9b: List of Questions for Treasure Hunting

Find as many of these treasures as you can in 20 minutes, using the people in this room as a resource. You are not allowed to get more than one answer from the same person, nor form groups of more than three at any one time. So keep moving around!

1. One person who was born the same month as you.

2. Two different ideas about how to help balance work and family life.

3. An excellent suggestion for how to build trust in a team.

4. An approach to managing the situation described below:

   Scenario: You notice that Fatma, a Somali refugee who has recently started working in the emergency-response team, is very quiet in staff meetings and never offers her own thoughts or opinions. You are concerned she will never advance if she cannot speak up. What would you do?

5. One thing about one of the following belief systems (or the experience of being part of that system) that will help you to be more sensitive to practitioners of those beliefs: Judaism, Hinduism, Buddhism, Christianity, Islam, Humanism, Atheism.

6. One thing learned by someone who has spent significant time overseas that has changed their life profoundly and has had a positive influence on their work.

7. A metaphor for working for the agency from someone who has been in the organisation for less than two years.

8. A metaphor for working for the agency from someone who has been in the organisation for more than five years.

9. A gem of wisdom about how to address poverty from someone who has experienced poverty directly.

10. One important perception about the beliefs, values, or behaviours that make the national culture you are currently working in different from other cultures.

Building Trust in Diverse Teams

Tool 10: Time lines

Learning objectives

The purpose of this tool is to:

- enable people to get to know each other and the significant events that have shaped their lives;
- encourage all team members to appreciate the gifts and qualities that each person brings to the team and to see the diversity of background, culture, and skills that are available in the team;
- help team members understand the values and motivations of their colleagues in the team.

Overview

For team members to trust each other, they need to know each other and understand each others' values and motivations. This tool helps to speed up the process of getting to know fellow team members, and can be done in the first or second week of the team life-cycle. For the time lines activity each team member plots events which have been significant in their lives on three different 'time lines' which are displayed around the room. The three time lines represent: 1) their personal lives (including family); 2) their working lives; and 3) their perception of key events in the outside world. Each of the three time lines stretches from the date of the birth of the oldest team member to ten years into the future, so that hopes and wishes for the future can also be included. At the conclusion of the exercise, each team member spends a few minutes explaining to the group why these events are significant for them.

Session plan

Overall time required	40 minutes plus 8 minutes per group member
Group size	10 –
Level of facilitation required	Medium
Relevant Trust Index items	Team composition Alignment Cultural
Resources required	Flip-chart paper and assorted coloured marker pens Masking tape or scotch tape Copies of Handout 10a: Links to the ten criteria for trust Copies of Handout 10b: Brief for Time Lines Activity

(NB Preparation for this exercise can be done in advance to save time on the day. Participants can either receive a verbal briefing or be given a written brief in advance so they can prepare before they come to the meeting. Also, the sheets of paper with the time lines on can be prepared before the participants assemble. To do this, the facilitator must know the approximate age of the oldest team member.)

How it works

1. Brief the whole group about the exercise.

2. Get the group to prepare three 'time lines' each on a separate large sheet of paper (or have them ready in advance). Each time line should be drawn to the same scale, using a ruler to measure off and mark ten-year intervals on a long line. The start date should be around the birth date of the oldest participant and the finish date should be ten years into the future.

3. Each of the time line sheets should be headed with one of the following headings:
   - Key Events in My Life
   - My Working Life
   - The Wider World

4. Place the three sheets with the time lines around the room, either on the floor in separate parts of the room, or on separate walls.

5. Hand out a brief for the time lines activity – one for each participant (a sample brief is given in Handout 10b). Emphasise that people need not reveal anything about themselves that they do not wish to share.

6. Ask participants to work on their own for 15 minutes to prepare their thoughts in accordance with Stage 1 in the brief.

7. When they are ready, ask the participants to visit each of the three time lines around the room and enter symbols that represent their thoughts, memories, and ideas. Suggest that they use the time scale to place the events at roughly the appropriate dates. Encourage them to use drawings or cartoons to illustrate each entry rather than relying on written words.

8. When everyone has made all their entries on the three separate sheets, bring the time line sheets together in one place, so that the dates on each sheet line up with each other.

9. Get the whole group to gather around the three sheets. Ask for a volunteer to go first. Then ask each participant in turn to tell their life story using the entries they have made on the time line sheets to explain why those things are of particular significance to them. Allow no more than ten minutes for each participant's story.

10. When everyone has had their turn, ask the group to reflect on and discuss the following questions:
    - What key themes and points of similarity emerge from the stories that have been told?
    - What differences in life experiences are noticeable?
    - What did you learn about differences in cultural background?
    - What have you learned about shared values within the team?
    - Identify one key quality/competence that the group most values about each person.

11. As a final step, ask the group to review the links to the ten criteria for trust (Handout 10a) while reflecting on the responses that other team members shared.

Facilitation tips

- Be sure to emphasise that nobody is being forced to reveal anything that they do not wish to share. However, explain that building trust requires taking some personal risks and so encourage people to be as open as they feel they can.

- Plain wallpaper or lining paper is ideal for this purpose and each sheet can be between 6–10 feet long depending on the space available. Alternatively, for each time line, three sheets of flip-chart paper on their sides and taped end to end with masking or scotch tape will work well. You could also use a large whiteboard/blackboard if available.

- As people tell their stories, model behaviour which values and appreciates both the content of what people say and also the fact that they are being open. Intervene with questions that show interest when appropriate and let other team members do the same. Be sure not to allow any behaviour that derides or belittles the story-teller.

- Make sure that everyone includes their thoughts about the next ten years for each of the three time lines. This can reveal a lot about their values, as well as their hopes and motivations.

Handout 10a: Links to the ten criteria for trust

Criteria	Definition	Impact of time lines
Competence	Trust based on a perception that team members are competent, and so will not let me down	The time lines activity enables team members to understand the skills and qualities that other team members bring to the team.
Reciprocity	Trust based on the observation that other team members are trusting and co-operative towards me	In taking part in this activity team members are, to some extent, allowing themselves to be vulnerable, and they all take this risk together.
Accessibility	Trust based on the fact that other team members share their true feelings and I can relate to them on a personal level	The time lines activity enables each individual to reveal personal things about themselves in a safe and protected environment. This helps team members get to know them better on a personal level.
Predictability	Trust based on the observation that the behaviour of team members is consistent over time and in different contexts	By seeing the key events that have shaped peoples' lives over time, it is easier to understand the attitudes and values that underlie their behaviour.

Handout 10b: Brief for Time Lines Activity

Introduction

This activity is designed to enable team members to learn about each other by sharing the significant events that have shaped their lives. You can decide what you share with the group. If some events are private and you do not wish to share them then do not feel you have to. Share only what you want to share.

Stage 1 – Reflection Time (15 minutes)

1. Please think back over *your life* and identify the people, places, and events which have:

    - had an important impact on you;
    - changed your views on life;
    - resulted in an important change in the direction of your life;
    - brought you great happiness or sadness.

    Make a note of the four or five most significant of these events and why they were important to you.

    Then project your thinking forward a few years and consider what you would like to happen to you (realistically!).

    Think about simple drawings or symbols that can represent important events or turning points in your life.

2. Now think about *your working life* and any organisations you have worked for. What have been the most important roles you have undertaken?

    - What did you learn in each of the jobs or roles you have undertaken?
    - What did you learn from your colleagues?
    - Who was the best boss you ever worked for and why? How did they influence you?

    Identify the key decisions you have taken about your working life and the changes you have made along the way – especially any that constituted a change of direction for you.

    Again project your vision forward, and think about what you would like to happen in your working life in the next ten years.

    Think about simple drawings or symbols that can represent important events or turning points in your working life.

3. Next, turn your attention to what has been happening in the *wider world* during your lifetime. This may be in your community, your country, or the world – whatever has struck you as important. Identify the events which have caught your imagination, and which you regard as significant, whether or not they have affected you personally.

    • What do you remember about the events?

    • Why do you think they were important?

    • What did you think and feel about them at the time? How do you feel about them now?

    • In this context choose one event that you would like to see happen within the next ten years and consider where you would place it on the time line.

Stage 2 – Sharing

When you are ready, enter the key events you have identified on the three time lines around the room. Use pictures, symbols, or key words to portray the events. Be ready to tell the other members of the team about your time lines and explain briefly why these things are important to you.

5 • Informal activities

Action research conducted in Sri Lanka and Malawi indicated that field managers and staff wanted ideas for less formal activities that would continue to build trust within their teams. Social activities are vital to help team members build stronger relationships, recognise achievements, boost morale, and foster a sense of team unity.

The purpose of the activities in this section is to strengthen team cohesiveness, and nurture trust within the team. This section includes ideas for ice-breakers, team social activities, and information about the new Global Diversity Board Game for International Relief and Development Organisations.

Save the Children

Save the Children staff gather with Bana Camp residents affected by the 2005 Pakistan earthquake to discuss a school rebuilding project.

Ice-breakers

Learning objective

The purpose of ice-breakers is to:

*   help staff to build relationships and share information in a fun and creative environment in a short amount of time.

Overview

Every staff meeting, team gathering, or workshop is an opportunity to foster stronger relationships between team members. Ice-breakers can be used during any team session. While short, they can go a long way to indirectly building trust in a team.

Session plan

A list of ideas for ice-breaker exercises is provided below. They are all short and should take anywhere from 10–20 minutes depending on the size of the group (with the exception of the carousel exercise which may take longer if the small-group activity is added at the end). Some of the ice-breakers are more physical than others; these can be good to use to generate some energy after lunch if you are holding a day-long workshop. As with sports activities, take into consideration different physical abilities of staff, including anyone with a disability, when selecting activities.

The ice-breakers are categorised by their main objective:

*   getting to know each other better
*   supporting one another
*   working together
*   creative thinking
*   aligning teams.

How it works

Select from the following ice-breakers depending on the nature of your team session:

Getting to know each other better

In terms of the ten criteria for trust, this group of ice-breakers tends to focus on swift trust, or trust based on competence, openness with information, integrity, and reciprocity.

Paper people: Everyone gets a piece of card or scrap of paper and lists three things about themselves: a) a physical trait, b) a personality trait, and c) an aspiration or thing they love to do. An alternative is to get everyone to write one thing about themselves that they think no one in the group knows about. All the scraps are put in a box, mixed up, and each participant pulls out a paper. Each one is read aloud, and the group must guess whom the paper is describing.

Two truths and a lie: Participants state three things about themselves, two true and one false, without revealing which is which. Other participants should try to discern which statement is the lie. Participants should be encouraged to be as creative as they can.

Supporting one another

In terms of the ten criteria for trust, this exercise promotes trust based on well-being and inclusion.

Circle of appreciation: This is an opportunity for team members who have worked together for a while to receive positive feedback from their team mates. Even if there is tension within the team, the facilitator should remind team members that there are always positive traits to recognise in everyone. Get everyone to sit in a circle, and provide each person with a sheet of paper. Ask everyone to write their name on the top of the paper. Then ask everyone to crumple up the paper into a ball. Tell them each to throw their balled-up paper into the centre of the circle. Ask each person to retrieve a paper ball and open it up. If they see their own name, they should trade papers with their neighbour. Ask each person to write down a positive trait or something they admire about the person named at the top of the paper. Have everyone ball up the piece of paper and throw it back into the centre of the circle. Repeat the steps above 5–10 times. On the final round, have someone pick up each piece of paper and hand it back to the person named on top. Each person should have 5–10 positive things listed about themselves.

Working together

In terms of the ten criteria for trust, these exercises promote trust based on openness with information and reciprocity.

Don't cross the line!: This game emphasises the importance of working together. Create a long line (with tape, string, draw it in the dirt, etc.) in the meeting area. Split participants into two groups and ask each group to place themselves on opposite sides of the line. Tell them that each group is going to get a special set of directions. Meet with Group 1 and secretly tell them that each of them is going to find a place on their side of the line and pair up with someone in Group 2 on the other side of the line. Their goal is to convince the person in Group 2, in whatever way they can, to cross the line and stand on the same side of the line as Group 1. Then move to Group 2 and provide them with the same set of secret instructions. Get the participants to place themselves on their side of the line. Shout 'Go!'. Give a few minutes for everyone try to reach their goal.

In trying to reach their goal, people will usually use various forms of coercion to convince their partner to cross to their side of the line. As the two groups' goals seem to compete with one another, some may resort to pulling or bribery. After a few minutes, call an end to the game. Ask people to share solutions that they found. See if anyone thought to share their instructions with the person opposite them, or if they kept them secret. Discuss the reasons for secrecy, aspects of trust (such as reciprocity-based trust), and the benefits of sharing goals up-front and finding ways to work together (for example, the pair can first stand together on one side of the line, and then on the other, meeting each other's goals.)

Write it/do it: Pairs of students sit back-to-back, and one student is chosen as the communicator and one as the listener. The communicator is given a simple line drawing (see overleaf for an example). The listener is given a piece of paper and a pen. The communicator must give clear directions to the listener so that the listener can draw the identical design from only the verbal directions given (for example, the communicator can say: 'Draw a medium-sized box in the middle of the paper…then draw…'). The listener cannot ask any questions for clarification and must remain silent. Compare the listener's drawing with the communicator's.

Continue with these same pairs and provide the communicator with a second drawing that is different from the first. Follow the same instructions, but this time the listener is allowed to ask questions of the communicator. Compare the two drawings.

Then ask these questions:

- How well did the communicator communicate? Did the communicator provide clear instructions? How could the communicator have improved?

- How did one-way communication compare to two-way communication?

- What did you find difficult about communicating information for the first drawing?

- Did it help to have the listener ask questions during the second drawing? Did you change your way of communicating as a result of the listener's feedback and questions?

Example drawing:

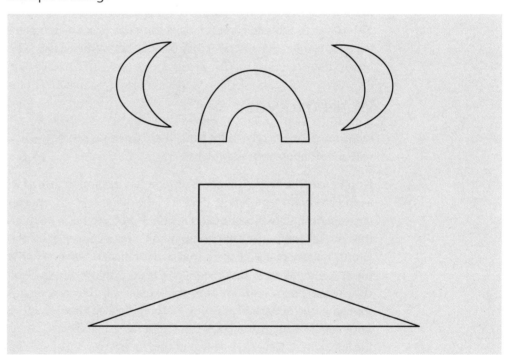

Ring of trust: Participants will have to negotiate and work together, initially with their eyes closed, in order to get themselves in a circle, joining hands. Some participants will naturally start to organise, others will not be able to move (due to entanglement) and will have to delegate and trust others to help. This activity is about realising the need to work together, trusting one another that each person will work effectively for a common purpose.

1. Ask the participants to stand in a large circle, close their eyes, and put their arms out in front of them.

2. Ask the participants to start to walk slowly in towards one another, keeping their eyes firmly closed. Facilitators are there to ensure there are no crashes, or poking of eyes!

3. Tell the participants that when they feel someone's hand they must hold it, and stop moving inwards. (Another option would be to allow participants to walk in towards each other with their eyes closed, and when you say stop, then to get them to hold onto any hands they feel at that moment.)

4. When each participant has joined a hand, or facilitators can do this for the loose hands, ask participants to open their eyes.

5. Tell participants that the object is now to move until they form a large circle, without breaking hands at any time. The circle should have no knots or twists in it.

6. Facilitators can help with suggestions.

7. After 10–15 minutes when the group have run out of ideas or started cheating, the exercise is complete.

8. De-brief: facilitators can perhaps ask participants how they felt, ask them to identify any skills they felt they used during the exercise, and whether these skills are relevant to any situations in which they interact with others.

9. You may need to adapt this activity for use in cultures where touching between men and women is not the norm. An alternative would be to carry out the activity in two different gender groups simultaneously.

Creative thinking

In terms of the ten criteria for trust, these exercises promote trust based on competence and openness with information.

Thinking outside the box: This is a fun physical activity to get participants moving, for example after a lunch break. It can also be used to help participants to get to know each other better. It is best used with a group of at least 12 people. Provide each person with a sheet of paper and ask them what shape it is (rectangle). Tell them that this game has one rule: that when they hear the whistle, each person must stand on (or get close to) a rectangle. Tell them that you will be asking a series of questions. They should find someone nearby to discuss the question with (in pairs, in threes, etc.). Questions can be related to the purpose of the meeting, but they could also be personal questions (such as 'what was your first job?' or 'how many people are there in your family?', etc.). The facilitator should have about five or six questions prepared.

Give the group about one minute to discuss the first question. While they are talking, quietly take away sheets of paper from one or two people. At the end of the minute, whistle to alert everyone to stand on (or get close to) a rectangle. People who do not have a piece of paper usually try to stand on other people's pieces of paper with them, or try to steal others' papers. Ask the second question, take more papers away, and sound the whistle again. After each question, as the facilitator removes more and more sheets of paper, it becomes increasingly challenging for everyone to 'stand on (or get close to) a rectangle' as they typically first think only of their sheet of paper. Participants will sometimes begin thinking of alternative solutions on their own. If not, prompt the group to begin thinking about the rules – to stand on a rectangle – does it have to only mean the piece of paper? The activity is best held in a rectangular room, preferably with floor tiles or in a rectangular field. Eventually someone will realise that a design in the floor makes a rectangle, the room is a rectangle, they can stand on or get close to a table, they can use a piece of flip-chart paper, etc. Remind everyone that even when things seem challenging, there is always a solution that can be found by thinking creatively and working together.

Carousel: This ice-breaker can be used for sharing ideas or information in pairs among a large number of people in a fast-paced, high-energy setting. It can prompt team members to share innovative ideas during strategic-planning sessions or to think creatively about solutions to a particular problem or issue. It can encourage team members to value one another's opinions and build competence-based trust. It is best for a medium to large group of 12–40 people. You need an even number of people to carry out this exercise.

1. Discuss with everyone the topic to be addressed during this exercise. It can be something such as: 'how do we encourage more community participation in our water and sanitation programme?' or 'what can we do to provide more social activities to staff to help build relationships and trust?'

2. Get everyone to stand in a big circle. Every other person should move inside the circle and turn around, facing those in the outer circle. In other words, there should be two circles with the outer circle people facing inward and the inner circle people facing outward, and everyone should be face-to-face.

3. Remind the group of the topic to be discussed and tell them to share as many of their ideas as possible with their partner, giving each person a chance to speak.

4. Each person should take notes and write down as many ideas as they hear.

5. Every 60 seconds, the facilitator should make a loud noise to signal that the outside person should move clockwise, and stand in front of the person to their left. It is important to keep the group moving fairly quickly, in order to keep the discussions brief and lively.

6. After 5–10 rotations, each person will have collected a long list of ideas. Get everyone to sit in small groups (4–5 people depending on total group size) and review all of the information they received. Each group should select the top three best solutions or ideas, write them each on a separate card, and post them on a board at the front of the room.

7. The group should review all of the cards, consolidate similar answers, and prioritise the various solutions or ideas presented.

(NB Steps 1–5 of this exercise can also be used to share personal information in order for team members to get to know one another better, by having each pair discuss a question regarding a personal topic rather than a programme-related topic. Steps 6 and 7 would be skipped.)

Proverbs: Participants search for the owner of the other half of their proverb, and then work with their partner to figure out what insight the proverb may offer about trust. Proverbs are common in many cultures around the world, and often quite amusing. Use the proverbs below or collect your own. Write half of each proverb on a separate slip of paper. Distribute the half proverbs to participants. Ask them to find their other half. Once they meet, ask them to figure out how their proverb might relate to trust. Offering a sample proverb and your interpretation of it can be useful.

Sample proverbs and suggestions about where to divide them:

A chain is only / as strong as its weakest link

If you neglect the pot / it boils over and extinguishes the fire

Even water can be held in a sieve / if you wait till it gets frozen

Softly, softly / catch the monkey

Don't climb the palm tree / with something in each hand

There is no better mirror / than a best friend

In confusion are / the seeds of understanding

A single bracelet / does not jingle

You only need to light one match / to spread the bushfire

Sweet and sour / go hand in hand

Aligning teams

These activities are slightly more involved and may take a bit longer than the others listed above. They help to address issues of team alignment and sharing a common sense of purpose. In terms of the ten criteria for trust, these activities address reciprocity, competence, and compatibility.

Visualise it: This exercise can be used when a team wants to set objectives for where it wants to be at the end of a relief effort. It is a fun activity using pictures and helps to unite teams around a common purpose.

1. Welcome the team and introduce the exercise. Explain that the purpose of the session is to generate consensus about where the team would like to be at the conclusion of a certain initiative.

2. Invite each team member to draw a picture on either an A4 or A3 size sheet of paper, that represents how they visualise the status of the emergency situation at the conclusion of the relief effort, at the conclusion of the recovery effort, or at a point two or three months from now.

3. Give each person about 15 minutes to complete their drawing. Emphasise that this is not an art contest.

4. When they have completed their picture of the future, invite them to draw a second picture that represents the current situation – the way it is today.

5. When the drawings are complete, ask each team member to present their pictures to the others. This can be done with both pictures presented at once or by having all the future pictures presented first and then the current situation pictures.

6. Encourage the team to ask questions during the presentations.

7. Facilitate a discussion at the conclusion of the presentations. Generate ideas on cards that capture the key shared elements of the desired future and then the key shared elements of the current situation.

8. Place the desired future statements on the right-hand side of a wall space and the current situation statements on the left, with a gap in between.

9. Quickly review the two sets of cards and ask the group (while pointing to the current situation cards): 'If this is where we are, and [pointing to the desired future] this is where we want to be, what are the main things we need to do as a team to bridge this gap?'

10. Note ideas that are shared by the team.

11. Ask what elements of trust are involved in getting the team across this bridge.

12. Again, capture the ideas that are shared.

13. Facilitate a discussion of the trust elements and get agreement on the three most important team actions that can be taken to ensure we arrive together.

14. Document the outputs and circulate to all team members.

© Dennis Hamilton, Managing Director, Training Associates Pacific.

What's your function?: This activity improves communication and understanding between two different teams and helps them to better understand one another's roles and responsibilities. The result of this exercise can be an increased sense of belonging to a larger effort and an understanding and appreciation of the work done by each team.

1. Bring the two teams together and even if they know each other, ask them to introduce themselves.

2. Get them to meet in their teams and discuss and outline what they understand to be the ten main functions of the other team. Each function should be written on a separate card.

3. Ask each team to present what they have written to the other team. No challenges should be allowed during the presentations, but questions could be asked to clarify what was being presented.

4. Get each team to take the list of functions that have been prepared by the other team, and meet to discuss the output. Functions that are accurate should be kept. If there are functions missing or incorrect, the team should write new functions on cards of a different colour.

5. Get the teams to come back together and then present their revised set of functions to the other. They should hold a discussion and elaborate on each of the functions listed.

6. Ask the members of each team to share what they learned from the sharing, what they appreciate about the work being done by the other team, and how they think it contributes to the overall relief and recovery work of the organisation.

Facilitation tip

> The ice-breaker concept may not be widely understood across all cultures, so you may need to provide an explanation before you introduce any of the activities.

Team socials

Learning objectives

The purpose of team socials is to:

* help team members get to know one another better and build stronger relationships;

* build a sense of common purpose and unity amongst team members;

* boost morale and motivation, and support the psycho-social well-being of staff.

Overview

In an intense emergency setting, a sense of urgency often leads to heavy workloads and long work hours. Focusing on actively responding to the emergency tends to take priority over making time to reflect and rejuvenate. But neglecting the latter is potentially harmful for individual health and successful team functioning. Services will be more effectively delivered if staff are able to take time out for rest and relaxation, establish good relationships with co-workers, feel appreciated for their hard work, and feel like a valued member of the organisation. It may seem self-serving to some to take time out in the midst of a serious emergency response to focus on themselves and their team, but even a short amount of time spent on team social activities will result in a more efficient and motivated team.

Session plan

A list of ideas for social activities is provided below. The most appropriate social activity for a given team can be selected depending on the stage of team development and the nature of the emergency setting. For example, day trips to another location to hold a meeting may only be possible once there is an improvement in the security level.

How it works

Forming a social committee

At least two staff are nominated to run a social committee. If the agency is small, the committee can be agency-wide. If the agency is large, with several large teams, a committee can be established within each team. The social committee collects information on birthdays, anniversaries, weddings, births, and holidays in the different team members' cultures. They can create a fun bulletin board highlighting these events, keeping it updated each month. If the team wants to celebrate these events, they can ask volunteers to help organise the celebration and to prepare enough food for all staff to participate. Each birthday can be celebrated, or monthly celebrations can be held for anyone having a birthday during that month. The social committee can also help celebrate a team success when a project milestone is reached.

Sharing a meal

In many cultures, eating together is an important aspect of building respectful relationships. If the agency has money available in the budget, it should host an agency-wide lunch or dinner. Otherwise teams can organise 'pot-luck' meals, where each team member brings a small amount of food or a drink to share with everyone. Offices should provide coffee and tea in the mornings and staff should be encouraged to take a few minutes to socialise with one another at this point. Ensure that food is made available equally among everyone, so that any perceptions of differences between team members are not exacerbated.

Day trips

Instead of holding a regular team meeting or planning session at the office, hold it off-site. Sometimes a simple change in location can help to stimulate more creative thinking and invigorate a team. For example, take the team to an 'away-day' at a pleasant location to hold an event such as a briefing or training session.

Sports teams

Sports encourage team building and promote physical and mental health. Agencies can set up intra- or inter-agency leagues. Usually volleyball, football (soccer), or kickball require the least amount of supplies and are easiest to organise. Ideas for sports activities should promote participation by both women and men, and take into consideration different physical abilities of staff, including anyone with a disability.

Agency choir or chorus

Just as sports teams bring together different people with common interests and create a sense of agency unity and pride, so can a singing group. Singing, as with sports, can also be an inexpensive way to let off steam. The group can hold regular practices and then perform at agency gatherings.

Team 'go and see' visit

Group trips such as visiting other programmes, for example, can be a way to encourage team learning and at the same time foster relationships and promote creative problem-solving. Often more than one agency is carrying out the same type of emergency-response programme, but in another location. Different agencies encounter similar types of challenges but may address them in different ways. Forming relationships and collaborating across agencies, although challenging, can provide mutual support and help to build trust both within a team and between agencies.

Links to the Trust Index

Alignment	Fun social activities involving all team members are organised on a regular basis to help staff build relationships
	Team successes are recognised and celebrated
	Team gatherings/communications help to develop and update a shared sense of purpose
Organisational	The well-being of staff is looked after. Adequate time off is ensured, stress-awareness materials are provided and discussed, psycho-social support is provided when needed

Global Diversity Board Game for International Relief and Development Organisations

The Global Diversity Board Game is a highly interactive training tool that uses a multiple-choice quiz format to explore facts about global diversity. It covers, for example, demographics, jobs, and society as well as how to effectively manage in a multi-cultural workplace. It is a thought-provoking game, adapted as part of the Building Trust Project especially for the international development sector, that highlights the importance of understanding differences and acts as a stepping stone towards building trust.

More information about the board game, and how to obtain copies is available at: www.ecbproject.org

Further resources

Covey, M. R. (2006) *The Speed of Trust*, New York: Simon & Schuster.

Doney, P. (1998) 'Understanding the influence of national culture on the development of trust', *Academy of Management Review*, July.

Emergency Capacity Building Project (2007) 'Building Trust in Diverse Teams: Scoping Study Report', available at: www.ecbproject.org/publications/ECB1/ECB_Building_Trust_in_Teams_Scoping_Study.pdf

Hurley, R. F. (2006) 'The decision to trust', *Harvard Business Review*, September.

Kourdi, J. and S. Bibb (2004) *Trust Matters: For Organisational and Personal Success*, Basingstoke: Palgrave Macmillan.

Sprenger, R. K. (2004) *Trust: the Best Way to Manage*, Cyan Campus.

Stephenson, Jr., M. (2005) 'Making humanitarian relief networks more effective: operational coordination, trust and sense making', *Disasters* 29 (4): 337–50.

Glossary

alignment	coming together behind a shared sense of purpose and/or common goal
appreciative inquiry	an investigative approach which focuses on 'what works', in order to bring about change
collectivist culture	a culture where the interests of the group are emphasised over those of the individual
high-context culture	a culture where context (what is between the lines or non-verbal) is more important than text (the explicit and direct use of words); a culture that is more interested in the quality of relationships within their context than in accomplishing tasks
high power-distance culture	a culture where it is accepted that there should be a large gap in terms of power and social status between managers and their staff
in-group	a group of people sharing similar characteristics, values, and approaches, producing feelings of community or solidarity
international staff	staff who are not from the country where the emergency is taking place
low-context culture	a culture where text (the explicit and direct use of words) is more important than context (what is between the lines or non-verbal); a culture where individual accomplishments are more important than the quality of relationships
low power-distance culture	a culture where it is perceived that gaps of power and social status between managers and their staff should be minimised
national staff	staff who are from the country where the emergency is taking place
orientation	a process to enable new employees to adjust to new surroundings, colleagues, and activities
out-group	a group of people perceived as other than / different from one's own
reciprocity	the quality of something being felt by both sides; mutual dependence (i.e. it is easier to trust someone else if we feel they are trusting towards us)